FEEDING YOUR FORGOTTEN SOUL

Spiritual Growth for Youth Workers

Zondervan/Youth Specialties Books

Adventure Games
Amazing Tension Getters
Called to Care
The Complete Student Missions Handbook
Creative Socials and Special Events
Divorce Recovery for Teenagers
Feeding Your Forgotten Soul (Spiritual Growth for Youth Workers)
Get 'Em Talking
Good Clean Fun
Good Clean Fun, Volume 2
Great Games for 4th-6th Graders (Get 'Em Growing)
Great Ideas for Small Youth Groups
Greatest Skits on Earth
Greatest Skits on Earth, Volume 2
Growing Up in America
High School Ministry
High School TalkSheets
Holiday Ideas for Youth Groups (Revised Edition)
Hot Talks
Ideas for Social Action
Intensive Care: Helping Teenagers in Crisis
Junior High Ministry
Junior High TalkSheets
The Ministry of Nurture
On-Site: 40 On-Location Programs for Youth Groups
Option Plays
Organizing Your Youth Ministry
Play It! Great Games for Groups
Teaching the Bible Creatively
Teaching the Truth about Sex
Tension Getters
Tension Getters II
Unsung Heroes: How to Recruit and Train Volunteer Youth Workers
Up Close and Personal: How to Build Community in Your Youth Group
Youth Specialties Clip Art Book
Youth Specialties Clip Art Book, Volume 2

FEEDING YOUR FORGOTTEN SOUL

Spiritual Growth for Youth Workers

Paul Borthwick

Zondervan Publishing House
Grand Rapids, Michigan

Feeding Your Forgotten Soul

Copyright © 1990 by Youth Specialties, Inc.

Youth Specialties Books, 1224 Greenfield Drive, El Cajon, California 92021,
are published by Zondervan Publishing House,
1415 Lake Drive, S.E., Grand Rapids, Michigan 49506

Library of Congress Cataloging-in-Publication Data

Borthwick, Paul, 1954-
    Feeding your forgotten soul : spiritual growth for youth workers / by Paul
Borthwick
        p.   cm.
    Includes bibliographical references
    ISBN 0-310-44421-7
    1. Church work with youth. 2. Spiritual life. 3. Borthwick, Paul, 1954- . I. Title
BV4447.B675   1990
248.8'92—dc20   90-32279
                                                                                      CIP

Edited by Noel Becchetti
Design and Photography by Mark Rayburn
Typography by Leah Perry

Printed in the United States of America

90 91 92 93 94 95 96 97 98 99 / AK / 10 9 8 7 6 5 4 3 2 1

ABOUT THE YOUTHSOURCE™ PUBLISHING GROUP

YOUTHSOURCE™ books, tapes, videos, and other resources pool the expertise of three of the finest youth-ministry resource providers in the world:

Campus Life Books—publishers of the award-winning *Campus Life* magazine, who for nearly fifty years have helped high schoolers live Christian lives.

Youth Specialties—serving ministers to middle-school, junior-high, and high-school youth for over twenty years through books, magazines, and training events such as the National Youth Workers Convention.

Zondervan Publishing House—one of the oldest, largest, and most respected evangelical Christian publishers in the world.

Campus Life
465 Gundersen Dr.
Carol Stream, IL 60188
708/260-6200

Youth Specialties
1224 Greenfield Dr.
El Cajon, CA 92021
619/440-2333

Zondervan
1415 Lake Dr., S.E.
Grand Rapids, MI 49506
616/698-6900

84/61

CONTENTS

Foreword
Acknowledgments

FOREWORD

There was a time when I believed that spiritual vitality was more or less automatic for people in the ministry; that it was the natural by-product of being a faithful servant of God. When God called a person into the ministry, I thought, he also somehow mysteriously transformed that person into a spiritual giant.

Boy, was I ever wrong. The truth of the matter is that ministry neither guarantees spirituality nor even necessarily encourages it. After dishing up ice cream for others all day, those who began their jobs as ice-cream lovers soon lose their desire to dish up any for themselves. What was once a passion becomes a drudgery.

Similar occupational hazards exist for youth workers in particular. Week after week youth workers dish up good advice for teenagers: how to resist temptation, how to deal with loneliness, how to build self-esteem, how to make friends, how to get along with family members, how to have a close relationship with God. But that advice—good as it may be for kids—after a while begins to blend into the background of the familiar, and one's taste for it begins to diminish, if it isn't lost altogether. A youth worker in that predicament no longer feels compelled to work at spiritual growth, to be faithful to God, to protect relationships, to guard personal integrity.

I know that this hazard exists because, to a degree, I have personally experienced it. Maybe you have too. I would venture to say that there are countless youth workers (as well as others in the Christian ministry) who struggle every day to keep their personal and spiritual lives in order while doing the Lord's work. Those who are unsuccessful in their struggle become discouraged, guilt laden, and spiritually dry, losing their effectiveness in the ministry. Some lead double lives—one that is public and another that is secretive and shadowy. Unfortunately, not a few of these people crash and burn—losing their faith, their ministries, their marriages, and even their lives.

Youth workers in the church are especially vulnerable to these dangers for several reasons, not the least of which is inexperience. Youth ministry is more often than not an entry-level position in the church, even though it is a ministry with great responsibility and importance. Further, youth workers are often viewed both by youths and adults as models of spirituality and Christian character for young people to emulate—an uncomfortable position for even the most mature Christian adult. Sometimes the pressure to live up to unreasonable expectations like these can produce burnout and extreme spiritual and personal dysfunction.

I have a good friend who often asks me how I'm doing. I usually answer by saying something to the effect that things are going fine—I'm keeping my head above water, the bills are getting paid, the job is getting done. But he will invariably persist by putting his hand over his heart and asking, "Yes, but how are things going in here? How are you doing on the inside?" I appreciate that question, even though it usually stops me in my tracks. It is a much more difficult question to answer, yet one we all need to be asked again and again. How are things on the inside? How is your heart? How is your soul?

Those are the kinds of questions dealt with in this exceptional book by Paul Borthwick. Paul knows that spiritual vitality is anything but automatic. He is well acquainted with the struggle for spiritual survival that all of us in youth ministry face; and he not only asks the important questions, but he provides practical solutions. In the first section of the book, he gives wise counsel on how to defend oneself against obstacles and temptations that destroy spiritual and personal integrity. He then outlines a sensible strategy for spiritual growth that is realistic and tailor-made for youth workers.

You have in your hands a very important book—perhaps *the* most important book ever written for youth workers. Please, don't take it lightly. Read it carefully and prayerfully. Take time to consider each point, writing your thoughts in the margins. Most of all, decide what you need to do *now* to "feed your forgotten soul," to rekindle your first love, and to remain spiritually alive. And remember: God is faithful. He will not let you down. "He who began a good work in you will carry it on to completion" (Phil. 1:6). If you desire a close relationship with God, he will be there for you. I trust that this book will encourage you as it has encouraged me.

Wayne Rice

ACKNOWLEDGMENTS

Any book is the product of a team, though only one person writes it. The materials I have written here are not uniquely mine, but are rather a result of the give and take of many relationships.

I am grateful to the many men and women who have served with me on the youth staff of Grace Chapel; they have been God's gifts of encouragement to me. From this group I am most thankful for Tim Conder, Jimmy Dodd, Tom McLaughlin, and Dan Mahoney, men who have stirred me up to love and good deeds.

I am also thankful for Doug Whallon and Steve Macchia, both of whom have served as on-site accountability partners; for Norman Nielsen, who never ceases to ask me how my quiet times are going; and for Duffy Robbins and Jim Burns, youth-ministry partners across the miles who have helped keep me honest and growing.

I thank God for the people at Youth Specialties and for their dedication to this project. I am especially thankful for Noel Becchetti, my editor, who helps to make me a better writer.

I owe my greatest debt to my wife, Christie, who has been God's gift of grace to me. She has helped me form my spiritual life, has endured with me through this writing project, and has lovingly confronted me whenever I wander from Jesus' pathway. I dedicate this book to her.

SECTION
ONE

THE HURDLES
TO
SPIRITUAL
GROWTH

WARNING: Veteran youth workers have determined that the side effects of youth work can be hazardous to your spiritual health.

When Rick drowned, my youth group reacted with grief, anger, and pain. How could such a great kid have his life snuffed out at age seventeen? Why would God let it happen? Their questions and needs taxed any pastoral skills I had acquired in my few short years of ministry leadership.

His body was not found for four days. Then there was the wake, the memorial service, and the burial. When I reached deep into my soul for the reserves needed to absorb the pain of others and offer a word of God's peace, the well was dry. I had been running on spiritual empty all year, and the crisis made me come to grips with my own superficiality and emptiness.

The youth group and I survived those difficult days, but the experience drove me into a period of searching. I wrote in my journal, "I used to be a good Christian. When I was in college, my spiritual disciplines—daily time with God, reading the Bible, personal witness to others—were all in good condition. I thought that full-time ministry would enhance my walk with Christ, but now, five years into it, I find that I am stale and spiritually out of shape."

Reflecting on the shallowness I saw in myself in that pressured situation, I wrote later, "Where did my spirituality go? I cannot remember ever actively rebelling against God, but after a few years into the ministry, I find myself growing distant from him. There's anger in me that I have never faced before, and I am headed toward becoming sarcastic and cynical."

Rick's death was not the cause of my spiritual drought. It merely revealed to me the state of my soul. It forced me to see that I had sacrificed my spiritual development in the pursuit of a successful ministry. I was setting a precedent that would put my picture in the dictionary next to the word "burnout." When I felt weary, I could not go on; I realized that I was running on empty, and I vividly saw my need to feed my forgotten soul. I wanted to move back to the point where I was serving others from an overflowing spirit, not an overtaxed one.

Through my years of exposure to youth ministry and youth workers, I have heard similar stories in various forms from a variety of youth workers. They have told of cruising along for years on old materials, worn-out stories, and spiritual charades, only to have their spiritual famine revealed through a crisis. A suicide, a car accident, getting fired, or a breakdown in relationships caused them to take a hard look at the state of their souls. Their experiences reeducated me on what I had learned earlier: Youth ministry can indeed be hazardous to our spiritual health.

We all get scared when, after a few (or many) years of service, we find ourselves sour or bitter or angry. We think about quitting the ministry or looking for a ministry in a new location. We hear of peers who left the faith, were unfaithful to their spouses, or simply burned out. We ask, How did this happen? And inside we ask, How can I prevent it from happening to me?

This is a book about preventive maintenance. Carefully guarding our own spiritual health and nurturing our spiritual growth are the best things that we can do to prevent burnout, spiritual apathy, or hostile withdrawal from God or ministry. We are looking for positive ways to feed our souls, not only to realize that we are hungry.

RESPECTING THE HURDLES

My roommate in college competed in the high hurdles on the University of Massachusetts track team. I occasionally watched the competitions, and I must admit I never had much respect for those hurdlers—that is, until I went down on the track during a practice one day and tried myself.

With a running start I could clear the first hurdle, but I looked more like a workhorse clearing a fence than the human gazelles of the track team. After a few strides I came to number two. With concentration I jumped it, but I had no steam left. The remaining hurdles were obstacles too large for me. I retired to the grandstand with a new respect for the race.

The spiritual race has many hurdles. For noninvolved spectators the obstacles may seem incidental; they may want to offer pat answers or easy solutions while they claim to be struggling over the hurdles. But for those of us in the race, the hurdles are very real. We may clear one or two with ease, but it is the repeated challenge that may knock us out of the race. We must have a respect for the challenges ahead and honestly evaluate how we can learn to overcome them.

TURNING ON THE LIGHTS

Before we look at exercises to get us in shape to face the hurdles, we need to understand the problems we face. There are issues in ourselves and themes inherent in youth ministry that trip us up in the race and leech our vitality from us. In the chapters that follow, we will shine the light on various pitfalls that may slow or even stop youth workers; but we'll also create a strategy for maintaining (or regaining) our spiritual stamina. As we look at problems, we will be forced to see ourselves not only as victims, but also (in some situations) causes of the spiritual malaise we can experience. We may be shocked to realize, along with the cartoon character Pogo, that "We have seen the enemy, and he is us!"

CHAPTER ONE
THE HURDLE OF MOTIVATION: WHAT'S DRIVING ME?

When 1984 began, my father was suffering from the long-term effects of a host of physiological problems. By early April he had been in the hospital seven times. On April 25 he died.

Later that week I began to process that information. My primary prayer supporter was dead. The man who had influenced me towards ministry was gone. Although I could not identify the issues yet, I began to struggle with the reality that one of the major reasons I had entered the ministry was removed. If I had entered Christian ministry just to please my father, I now had no reason to stay.

The other major human reason I had entered ministry—our senior pastor, Gordon MacDonald—was removed later that year. In September he resigned; by November, he was gone. By the end of 1984, I found myself dealing with my sense of purpose, my call to youth ministry: *Why was I in the ministry— and in youth ministry—in the first place?*

OPENING THE FLOODGATES

Asking questions about the influence these men had on me led to increased evaluation, doubting, and self-interrogation. I began to wrestle with such questions as: Am I in youth ministry to serve God? Or do I just like the status and power it gives me over those younger than I? Did I take the job simply because no one else wanted it—reasoning in my negative self-esteem that at least I was better than nothing? Could it be (as some sociologists assert) that I undertook youth-ministry leadership to fulfill a latent desire to obtain the popularity that I always wanted in high school?

As I evaluated I shuddered to realize that I could not discount any of these as motivators. I wanted to please my father and my pastor. I did feel superior to the kids. I wondered if I could do so-called real ministry. I enjoyed my status among the students. Although I hated to admit it, my own immaturity, ego, and insecurity had been woven deeply into my sense of call. I was forced to start the process of reevaluation because I realized that if my primary motives went unchecked, *I* could be my greatest obstacle to future spiritual growth.

> *Errant motivations distract us from the*
> *fundamental spiritual question, What is Jesus'*
> call *on my life?*

WHO CAN STAND?

If we evaluate our reasons for being in youth ministry and we find that a host of unspiritual incentives got us here, what then? While recognizing mixed motives does not disqualify us from eventual effective growth (and effective youth-ministry leadership), we must see the problems before we can move forward.

If I am motivated by a desire to succeed, my expectations will be directed towards notoriety, the opinion of others, and a comparison of my ministry against others. If these are my expectations, then my performance in leadership will be directed towards winning applause. If my performance in leadership is to gain applause, then my spiritual health will be sacrificed in favor of calling attention to my external performance.

Consider the examples of two real-life youth workers (their names and some identifying details have been changed).

Al's motivation is to be a successful youth worker. This need to achieve arises partly out of a feeling that he is not a success as a person, a feeling exaggerated by his unaffirming father. For Al success means big programs, big numbers of students, and being the best. Al reveals his inner drive when he jokes, "When Jesus said, 'Feed my sheep,' he really meant, 'Count my sheep.'" Al's expectations affect the way he leads. He is very task-oriented, secretly pleased when people call him a workaholic. He is a recruiter, a planner, an administrator, and an all-around ringmaster. Unfortunately, over time Al has degenerated into a very superficial person. He measures everything by externals: how many, how big, how awesome.

Al suffers spiritually. He is trying to be all things to all people, but feels that he is burning out and cannot keep up. Veteran youth worker Les Steele describes Al well: "We fall into the performance trap [because] we do not have a good sense of our own identity. If we enter the ministry to find ourselves rather than out of a clear sense of self, our identity is shaped by all the different people who have something to say to us."[1]

Al has sacrificed his spiritual health to his perception of productivity and success. He has given himself to a faulty goal, and he is being swallowed up. Yet Al will have difficulty getting over this hurdle if he does not recognize that he is a big part of this problem. "If our work is swallowing us up," writes author John Sanford, "it may be that we *want* to be swallowed. To solve this problem we must look into ourselves to discover what inadequacies or what personal needs in us we are trying to cover up by our immersion in work."[2]

Unlike Al, Mike is much more of a relational person. He is strongly motivated by his desire to be liked by his students. He admits that he was a nerd in high school, and youth ministry has afforded him with greater popularity than he ever had in his teen years. Mike wants to be cool; he wants students to say, "You're just like us; you understand us." His strength is relationships, and he pours himself into building bridges to students.

If Al is a high-task person, Mike is a high-touch person. He works hard to build comradery, hangs around with students, and truly identifies with them. Discipline and a challenge to maturity are conspicuously absent from his ministry.

Mike suffers spiritually because he strives to be true to a false self. Mike is twenty-eight, married, and has a child on the way, yet he spends most of his free moments with students who "need" him. Since he measures effectiveness by closeness to his students, his spiritual growth (as well as his ability to relate to adults—as his wife will testify) has been stunted.

Mike suffers from what Dr. Dan Kiley called the Peter Pan Syndrome. Like Jerry Rubin, who exclaimed in the sixties, "We're gonna be adolescents forever!" Mike has made a strategic, relational decision that will eventually hamper his long-term effectiveness. As an eight-year-old might return to thumb-sucking, Mike is trying to re-create through youth ministry a happier or more stable time of life.

His need to be liked by students waters down whatever prophetic function he might have had in their midst. The day is coming when the students' perspective will jump from, Isn't Mike a cool guy who identifies with us? to, When is Mike gonna grow up?

SO, WHAT CAN WE DO?

We all must recognize that a host of pure and impure motives contribute to where we are today. In my own ministry, youth mission teams have become somewhat of a forte. Once after speaking on the subject, I was approached by a thoughtful young woman who asked, "Are you convinced of the effectiveness of these teams, or are you just giving teenagers experiences you wish you had when you were in high school?" I paused before telling her I didn't know. After all, I never flew on an airplane until age twenty-four (but I now had in the youth group mature seventeen-year-olds who had flown thousands of miles while ministering on four continents), and my family, though not poor, could never have afforded to send me on one of our mission trips.

I decided she was at least partly right. I was experiencing vicariously through our teams a teenage life that I never had. If she were to ask me the same question today, I would tell her that I believe those teams were effective, *and* I believe I was partly motivated by selfish desires. The good news is this: In spite of the impurities, God—by grace—still worked through me. Youth workers who lead because of a desire to be successful, to be liked, or to be powerful may still carry out effective ministries, at least short-term.

But over the long haul, faulty motives will not endure. My desire for vicarious adventure through our students could keep me going two or three summers, but after that my motivation (or call) would wane. Tony Campolo, sociologist and nationally recognized speaker, points out that "many youth workers enter the ministry to satisfy emotional needs that characterize immaturity. As they outgrow these immature emotional needs which they have gratified in youth ministry, they find that youth ministry loses the capacity to excite them."[3]

Spiritual growth and health can be enhanced only when we are willing to go back to Jesus with regularity and evaluate: Why am I here? What am I living for? What would I die for? As we process our answers to these questions, we find spiritual renewal in our sense of call. An unwillingness to examine our motives may allow us short-term effectiveness in youth ministry, but eventually, as our spiritual growth suffers, we will quit. The hurdle of long-term motivation will be too much for us to face.

Evaluating our fundamental motives for entering youth ministry can be threatening, but it is a helpful start if we are to "put a wedge in the revolving door"[4] of youth-ministry leadership.

TAKE FOUR AND CALL ME IN THE MORNING

In his book *The Seven Habits of Highly Effective People*,[5] managerial consultant Stephen Covey relates the story of renewal in the life of author Arthur Gordon. Gordon, feeling a personal malaise about life and finding himself unmotivated, went to see a physician. The physician found nothing wrong, so he asked Gordon, "Will you follow the instructions I will give you for one day?" Gordon agreed. The doctor instructed him to go to a place of sanctuary, a beach where he had often gone as a child, and to take only food (no books, radio, or other interferences). The doctor told him to open four prescriptions—at 9:00 a.m., noon, 3:00 p.m., and 6:00 p.m. The four prescriptions read as follows:

9:00 a.m. Listen carefully. (Three hours just to listen—to the sea, to the birds, to himself, to God.)

Noon. Try to remember. (Three more hours to harken back to childhood, to identify the contributing factors that had made him the man that he was today.)

3:00 p.m. Examine your motives. (The hardest three hours because it forced him to come to grips with negative drives within himself that were keeping him from the fulfillment of serving others.)

6:00 p.m. Write your worries in the sand. (A helpful exercise to show him that, like the tide over the sand, God can erase our concerns.)

The four prescriptions from that doctor would be good for all of us when we examine our own call to ministry.

PROACTIVE RESOLVE #1 _____

Spiritual health demands that we face ourselves and the
hurdle of our mixed motives honestly. As we confess and
repent of errant motives, Jesus will renew our long-term
sense of call to him and to his work.

CHAPTER TWO
THE HURDLE OF SUCCESS: WHAT AM I STRIVING FOR?

I was in Philadelphia attending my first-ever youth-workers convention. As I entered the elevator, I was feeling pretty good about our youth ministry.

It was then that a youth worker I had never met before introduced himself. We exchanged niceties, and then he asked forcefully, "So, Paul, what is your vision for evangelizing the campuses in your area? How many students have you personally led to Christ this year? Do you have a strategy?"

We arrived at my floor, and I bid him farewell after only mumbling a few dull responses to his pointed questions. On an elevator ride of seven floors, I had been reduced from feeling affirmed to feeling like a total failure. I did not have the right answers for this man. He had hit me at our ministry's weakest point—evangelism.

I went back to the room to do some hard thinking. The challenge from my aggressive friend was appropriate for two reasons. First, it delivered me from a complacent feeling that my youth ministry was satisfactory in all respects. But the second impact of that conversation was more significant: His challenge got me thinking about success. What is success? Is it doing everything that speakers and seminar leaders say I should be doing? Is it having a strategy to evangelize the campuses in my area?

The conversation, difficult as it was, reminded me of a book by Robert Raines, *Success Is a Moving Target*. Why do we fail spiritually? Because we sacrifice our spiritual lives in pursuit of what we perceive to be success. That moving target called success introduces us to the second hurdle in our spiritual growth.

We lose our spiritual direction when we make it our priority to pursue the elusive target called success.

KNOCKED DOWN BY SUCCESS

Imagine a hurdle that increased 12 inches in height at the moment the runner attempted to straddle it. It would knock him down or completely out of the race! That's the way it is with success. Just as we think we can attain the goal that we think will make us feel successful, it shoots up and blocks us. The pursuit of success cries for more—a few more students, a few more programs, a few more verses memorized, a few more goals achieved. David Rockefeller, one of the wealthiest men in the world, illustrated it when he was asked, "How much money is enough?" He responded, "A few thousand dollars *more*."

Pursuing success knocks us down spiritually because it makes us feel like failures. "One of the main deceptions we tend to believe," writes Robert McGee, "is that success will bring fulfillment and happiness. Again and again we've tried to measure up, thinking that if we could meet certain standards, we would feel good about ourselves. But again and again we fail, and we are left feeling miserable. Even if we succeed almost all of the time, occasional failure can be so devastating that it can dominate our perception of ourselves."[1]

In a youth worker's seminar I led, I asked the question, "In twenty years, what would need to be true for you to look back and say, 'I have been a success'?" One young man responded, "If the students I am working with today are still walking with the Lord, then I have been successful. Their ongoing faithfulness is the measure of my effectiveness."

Listeners sighed with admiration at this measurement. Who doesn't want to be like John the apostle, finding joy to hear of our "spiritual children" walking in the truth (2 John 4)? My mind flashed to Jeff and Glenn, missionaries in Japan, to Tom in seminary, to Holly in youth-ministry leadership, to Elaina finishing her master's degree in social work. When I thought of the students I had worked with five to ten years earlier, I felt like a success by his definition.

But then I remembered others. Students from my ministry, including even those who had served on our discipleship-focused missions teams, who now suffered from alcohol dependency, whose marriages were in shambles, who had committed suicide, whose faith had been left at the high-school graduation ceremony as they went off to become party animals. My thoughts of these students dissipated any thoughts of success that I had entertained earlier. My mind roamed to thoughts of spiritual failure: Who was I to think that I had had *any* impact on others?

Pursuing success knocks us down spiritually because we get caught in the cycle of comparison. James and Mary Tillman wrote a thought-provoking book on racism titled *Why America Needs Poverty and Racism*. In the book they argue that many of the "isms" (race, class, and sex, for example) are built on the American way of identity formation at someone else's expense. A poor white person finds peace because "At least I'm not black," and a middle-class black person finds peace because "At least I'm not poor." The basic idea is expressed in the Pharisee's prayer: "God, I thank you that I am not like other men—robbers, evildoers, adulterers—or even like this tax collector" (Luke 18:11).

The cycle fails, however, because our comparisons downward ("at least I'm not like . . . ") are overshadowed by those over us. If I feel successful because I have written several books, I can feel superior by comparing myself to others who have written no books. But what do I do with my friend Jim Burns who has written five times my total? The comparison cycle draws me like a fly into the spider's web. "Well," I reason, "maybe he has ghost writers or a research staff." As I try to defend my self-esteem, now shaky because I am not as successful as I thought, I rationalize by making myself equal to those who are conspicuously more successful than I.

And we do it in youth ministry. If we feel successful because our youth group has the best program in town—the hottest mission trip, the biggest rally—we are setting a standard of success based on comparison, and this will lead either to pride or to despair.

The pursuit of success knocks us down spiritually because it creates false images of successful people. At one of my first youth-ministers gatherings, I went to every seminar, notebook in hand, hungry for the keys to effective Bible study, the best methods of youth discipleship, the design for effective youth-ministry talks, and the sure-fire solutions to mobilizing church kids. I listened. I took notes. I gobbled it up.

But two weeks after the conference, I felt depressed. I had learned the keys to effectiveness (or so I thought) at these seminars, but I couldn't seem to implement them. Fortunately, an older, more experienced youth worker helped me process my perceived failure: "You are suffering under the illusion that every one of the speakers you heard is implementing every one of the ideas you learned. Chances are, the woman who spoke on youth-group discipleship does that very well, but her Sunday-school program might be nil. The man who spoke on effective youth talks—how does he organize a retreat?"

His point made sense. The specialists in each area made me feel (although unintentionally) that unless in *every* area of my ministry I were as successful as they were in their specialization, I was a failure. I have since learned that there are no superhero youth workers. Even the most successful in one area might be a dismal failure somewhere else.

Setting up others as images of success gives us false expectations of our ministries. Exciting speakers can amuse and challenge us through their stories of God at work in their ministries. We hear them and wonder, Why is my ministry so dull? Marilyn Laszlo, Wycliffe Bible translator in Papua, New Guinea, came to speak at our church several years ago. She told some great stories—some made us roll with laughter, and others brought tears to our eyes. I was determined to listen to her as often as I could.

After about five messages, I noticed that Marilyn began to repeat her stories. She had eight, maybe ten, great stories. Then I calculated that with fifteen-plus years in New Guinea, Marilyn was averaging less than one great story per year. The rest of her ministry was obscure, unentertaining, hard work. Knowing that gave me courage to persevere in youth ministry because it made me face the reality that most ministry is not one nonstop success story after another; it is God at work through our faithful endurance.

The pursuit of success knocks us down spiritually because it leaves us at the mercy of others' opinions. For most of us, success is determined more by what others say about us than by what we feel about ourselves. If this is true, we are in for a roller-coaster ride because the feedback we get from others is seldom uniform. In fact, Jesus warns us to beware if everyone speaks well of us (Luke 6:26).

As youth pastor I was often given other ministerial responsibilities to help broaden my experience. On one occasion I was leading a service at a nursing home. Since they expected me to look pastoral, I had donned a sport coat—a brown plaid that I considered my best—and tie for the occasion. I led the service, gave a brief devotional, and closed in prayer. Most of the attenders filed out mumbling something like, "Thank you, Reverend," or, "Nice service, Pastor," under their breath. I suppose I was feeling a little smug about my versatility—able to speak to a nursing-home audience by day and to enthusiastic teenagers by night.

A spunky looking lady in a wheelchair rolled towards me. She seemed harmless, so I prayed (pridefully), "God, help me to handle affirmation without pride." I grasped both of her hands, as our Minister of Pastoral Care would have done, and gave her a warm greeting. "Young man," she said sternly, "I *never* thought I would live to see the day when a minister would wear a coat like that!"

And she wheeled away.

In one short comment she reduced the versatile youth minister to a blight on the ministry. If our posture in ministry depends on the commentary of others, we will either find ourselves distracted in search of the praises of men and women or devastated by those who criticize us. Ultimate spiritual success is getting God's approval, not others'.

The pursuit of success knocks us down spiritually because it leaves us unfulfilled when we do achieve it. My wife and I were flying home from Singapore. By a miracle of God, we were sitting in business class, returning home from a conference of three hundred leaders from seventy countries. Youth leaders and pastors present at the conference gave accounts of God's miraculous works in countries we had only heard about. We had been two of forty Americans invited. The invitation, the business-class travel, the conference, and the people we met were a dream come true.

The experience gave us feelings of external success, but it mattered little at that point. During the conference we had called home twice. On the first call we learned that our senior pastor's five-year-old daughter had leukemia. The second call brought more bad news: A dear friend had resigned his Christian leadership position because of an adulterous affair. What did superficial success matter in the face of Kristen's leukemia? Who cares about international networks of new friends when my old friend is at one of the lowest points of his life? The feelings of success were short-lived because we saw other realities that put our lives in perspective.

After the Dallas Cowboys won the Super Bowl, Cliff Harris, the safety, described his feelings: "You have something to look forward to only if you lose. After we won I looked over at Charlie Waters and whispered, 'But whom do we play next?' When you win the Super Bowl—I hesitate to say it—you're depressed."[2]

Success is not all that people make it out to be. Realities of life temper it (as in our case) or feelings of loss force us to re-evaluate (as in Cliff Harris' case).

The pursuit of success knocks us down spiritually because it distracts our focus. On many days I know that I've cheated my wife out of time together because I had to make one extra phone call or spend a few extra minutes in preparation. In my desire to be successful, I strove to care for others while ignoring the person I care about most. When success becomes the goal, other priorities are pushed into second place. Youth minister Kent Keller instructs those who "want" to burn out in youth ministry—in their search for success—to "make sure you stay so busy you don't have time for God. A good formula to follow is to spend ninety-eight percent of your time and energy running around telling kids how wonderful it is to have a personal relationship with God, leaving two percent of your time and energy for your own relationship with Him."[3]

Keller's tongue-in-cheek advice highlights the greatest pitfall of the pursuit of success; it distracts us from what should be our top priority—our relationship with God. Even the goal of Christian growth should be secondary to this relationship. As soon as we are preoccupied with our own progress as Christians, we take our eyes off of Jesus and put them on ourselves. Honoring Christ should be our foremost priority.

When worldly success dominates our thinking, we focus our attention on power. We try to orchestrate situations to put ourselves in the best light, rather than simply serving and leaving our reputations in God's hands. The temptation to be successful is the third temptation of Jesus. After showing Jesus all the kingdoms of the world and their splendor, the Devil said, "All this I will give you if you will bow down and worship me" (Matt. 4:9). "Circumvent God's way, sacrifice your priorities, and I will give you success beyond belief," says the Devil—to Jesus and to us.

YEARBOOKS
FOR CHRIST

Urban specialist Buster Soaries tells the story of his chagrin one day when he learned of an effective youth worker who had left his position at a large church to go sell high-school yearbooks. Buster assumed that burnout must have caused him to leave the ministry. When Buster approached him to discuss his decision, Buster found that he talked excitedly about his "new ministry." He said, "Buster, do you realize how many high-school campuses I will be able to reach for Christ by selling yearbooks?" Buster then describes his response to the young man's fervor.

> I looked at him with a new respect that approached awe. He was starting an outreach in places where he would not have been welcome as a youth pastor. My friend was

obviously more committed to the cause of Christ than to his success at a large church.

Suppose there was a way I could make a greater impact for Christ doing less glamorous work. What would I choose? Many of us are so excited about what we do that we easily fall into the trap of forgetting why we do it. Our success can then become our downfall.[4]

Buster Soaries' friend had his eyes on the prize. He was not trying to cross the hurdle the world calls success. He sought faithfulness in following Jesus. God does not call us to success. He calls us to faithfulness. Paul wrote to the Corinthians, "So then, men ought to regard us as servants of Christ and as those entrusted with the secret things of God. Now it is required that those who have been given a trust must prove *faithful*" (1 Cor. 4:1-2).

Faithfulness is difficult, but it is not impossible. As we commit ourselves to spiritual growth and health, we need to make sure that we are pursuing God's best for us—namely, faithfulness to him.

PROACTIVE RESOLVE #2 _____

Spiritual health means relinquishing our desire for success and refocusing our energies on faithfully knowing and following Jesus Christ.

CHAPTER THREE
THE HURDLE OF LONELINESS: AM I ALL ALONE?

The trip to Africa was a dream come true. We had ministered in South Africa, visited missionary friends in Mozambique, and gotten exciting glimpses of four other countries. Christie and I were elated after the trip. Ten days after our return, however, the elation ceased. We got word that Christie's Mom had been taken to the hospital. The first night we went to the emergency ward and sat. Then came the first operation, the second, the emergency amputation, the respirator, and much more.

The support of our families was outstanding, but during those first two weeks, we wished that our friends would come by. We didn't care if they had anything to say; we just wanted them to come and sit by us. We rationally knew about their busy schedules, the distance they would have to drive, and the awkwardness of coming to the hospital, but our emotions cried out for company.

During these difficult days, I found personal comfort in the account of Elijah's battle with loneliness and depression. He, too, was coming off a dream-come-true experience. He must have been elated over what was probably the greatest spiritual victory of his life—the defeat of the prophets of Baal. God had demonstrated his power with an awesome, stone-consuming fire from heaven.

After the spiritual high of winning the battle, however, he became acutely aware that the war was not over. His enemies were still after him, and he feared for his life. Ahab's witch-of-a-wife, Jezebel, who wants revenge for what Elijah did to her prophets, says, "Elijah, I'm coming after you!"

Elijah runs for his life into the desert. There, tired and hungry, he decides to call it quits. "He came to a broom tree, sat down under it, and prayed that he might die. 'I have had enough, Lord,' he said. 'Take my life; I am no better than my ancestors' " (1 Kings 19:4).

Elijah falls into the sleep of depression, but God strengthens him, first by sleep, then by food, more sleep, more food. By verse eight Elijah is ready for a superhuman journey, but exhaustion again takes over. Elijah retreats to a cave where God comes after him. In verses ten and fourteen, Elijah expresses to God the ultimate reason for his despair: "I am the only one left, and now they are trying to kill me, too."

We do not get to hear the tone of Elijah's voice as those words were spoken. Was he whining? Complaining? Were his words full of self-pity, uttered to God to say, "Why don't you do something?" Whatever the tone, we know that Elijah wanted to quit because of exhaustion, fear (he sensed the threat), and loneliness (he found no support). The first two would have been easily overcome if Elijah had had some compatriots.

When we sat in the waiting room, we were emotionally drained, and we faced an uncertain future with fear; but our loneliness was magnified because no one came to sit with us. When Moses grew tired at the battle, Aaron and Hur held up his arms. When David was threatened, he drew strength from his band of mighty men. But to be alone magnifies all other problems. Perhaps this is why God removes neither the threat nor the exhaustion from Elijah. Instead, he tells him that he is not alone. There are seven thousand in Israel who have not compromised themselves in the worship of Baal.

Of all of the hurdles in youth ministry, aloneness can be the most overwhelming, especially to those of us who tend to be melancholy. We, too, want to sit under a tree and say "It is enough" to God.

When I was first in youth ministry, I listed all of the biblical characters I thought suffered from loneliness and depression. I came across:

- Job—alone on the ash heap.
- Moses—forty years away from his people in Egypt, forty years alone tending sheep, forty years of controversial leadership while wandering in the desert.
- Elijah—the only one left.
- David—forsaken by his sons.
- Jeremiah—whose lamentations are the cries of a young man who senses he is alone in following God: "It is good for a man to bear the yoke while he is young. Let him sit alone in silence, for the Lord has laid it on him" (Lam. 3:27-28).
- Esther—alone in facing the King of Persia.
- Mary—a teenage mother who must have wondered, Who will believe my story?
- Jesus—abandoned at the hour of his deepest need.
- Paul—alone at the beginning of his ministry, alone at the end.

If we feel alone in the challenges of spiritual life or the youth ministry, we have good company. The great men and women of faith have gone before us and crossed this hurdle.

We lose perspective of spiritual priorities because we feel we are all alone in the challenges we face.

SO TIRED OF BEIN' ALONE

Spiritual progress grinds to a halt when we become preoccupied with being isolated or alone. We face the choice: Will we use that sense of aloneness to bring us toward God, or will

41

we separate ourselves from him? I can tell when I am succumbing to the negative response when I observe the following traits in myself.

Complaining. A fellow youth worker and I were sitting together in a sandwich shop, discussing our youth groups. Actually, we were playing a game of "Can you top this?" with stories of how poorly we were treated by youths, parents, and the church. In the midst of our conversation, an older man who had obviously been listening ventured past us. He stopped at our table and asked, "I want to know—do you *love* the people you work with?" With that rebuke, he left.

His point was clear. If we really loved these people, why were spending all of our time complaining about them? Did we know that love covers a multitude of sins? Had we forgotten that love bears all things?

Our conversation resulted partly from a sense of aloneness. My youth-worker friend and I enjoyed being together because we felt that our mutual ministries allowed us to understand each other. We got together because misery loves company. Using our sense of aloneness as justification, we made the error of excusing bad behavior and careless conversation. Complaining hides the state of our spirits, and rather than dealing with the loneliness within, we grow cynical or bitter towards others—or even towards God.

Self-pity. At one of my lowest points several years ago, I was thinking Elijah-like thoughts about myself and my ministry. I was ready to tell God that it is enough. Several partners on our staff team had departed, and a number of my closest friends in the ministry had left the church.

I must interject at this point that I am a wallower. When feeling melancholy, I can wallow in self-pity mud with the best of the pigs. I can take tiny mole hills and create huge mountains out of them. I can convince myself that one bad comment discounts a thousand good ones and that anything good that has ever come from my life came by luck. I listen to sad music and exaggerate my woes.

My wife is not so. She is more likely to say, "Okay, we're down, but let's shake the dust off of ourselves, get back up, and move on!" We are a good blend; she has taught me to identify self-pity for what it is—sin. But there have been times of tension when I could not dust myself off quite as quickly as she thought I should.

At a time when I felt acutely alone, I went to a Christian bookstore. Looking for something to salve my emotional wounds, I found the book *The Friendless American Male*. Now, several years later, I note that I still have not read the book. Why? Because I purchased it simply out of self-pity. I was feeling like a friendless American male, so I pampered myself rather than going to God, who could have opened my eyes to the dozens of people who were still partners with me. Spiritual maturity means looking up to see God's provision rather than concentrating on our own feelings of loneliness.

Blaming. I have a relative who suffers from advanced paranoia. It is a sad, crippling state of mental illness, but occasionally, even in his confusion, he manages to teach us all something profound about ourselves. One day we were asking him why he was not going to leave the house. He made all sorts of excuses, but finally said, "It's them—out there." He pointed in the general direction of the street. When we asked who they were, he simply repeated, "It's them—out there." He would not leave the house because of them—out there. He hid in the house with the shades pulled down and the curtains drawn tight because of anonymous others. *They* made him afraid. *They* were out there. There's nothing wrong with me—it's *them*.

When my spiritual life is stagnating, my first instinct is to find someone to blame. When I am at a point of spiritual dryness or emptiness, I look for my own assortment of "thems out there" that I can blame. I entertain such thoughts as these:

If only these church people wouldn't demand so much of me, I could have more time for spiritual growth.

If the pastor would give time to discipling me, I would be able to grow. With the little attention he gives me, it's no wonder I'm just drifting along.

If these kids would show more spiritual interest, it would sure make my growth easier.

Some or all of these statements might be true. But they are not excuses to stagnate spiritually. When all is said and done, the only person I can hold fully responsible for my spiritual growth or spiritual stagnation is me! Business consultants call this the difference between being reactive (blaming others for my state of affairs) and proactive (doing whatever I can in spite of the apparent problems). When I spend my time blaming "them out there," I am reacting and not taking responsibility for my own life. If I want to excuse my own spiritual mediocrity, I can blame others, or I can look proactively to the heart of the matter: myself.

Discouragement. Self-pity occurs when we overlook the resources that God has given us and, in the face of challenges, we decide to give up. When there seem to be no resources, when the challenges seem insurmountable, we feel like Job or Elijah or Jeremiah or Jesus—totally alone. There are no easy answers for genuine discouragement. Elijah needed a good meal and some rest, but that is a trite response for the solitary youth worker who finds no rest in the face of seemingly hopeless situations.

Mother Theresa, though not a youth worker, offers us a model of response in the face of hopelessness. In her work among the destitute and dying in the awesome city of Calcutta, India, she rises with her Sisters of Mercy for two hours of quiet devotion each day. She waits on the Lord, asking him for the strength needed to face each new day.

In the face of discouragement, perhaps the only solution is to wait. Wait on the Lord; staying in his presence (as Elijah eventually did) offers scriptural promise of restoration and rejuvenation (Isa. 40:31; Psa. 91). Time in God's presence can renew perspective and invigorate us to return to the battle.

In the face of discouragement, we can quit or give up hope too early. This may have been what happened to Demas. Perhaps he grew too discouraged with the opposition and imprisonments, and he threw in the towel. Paul writes, "Demas, because he loved this world, has deserted me" (2 Tim. 4:10). If only he had waited.

Visiting Hours are Open. In the face of Elijah's aloneness, God revealed the seven thousand others who were his partners. The threats continued, and the exhausting days of ministry wore on, but Elijah was renewed to hear of the other band of faithful followers who were engaging the evil powers with him. In specific response to Elijah's need, God directed him to Elisha, who would become first his understudy, then his successor.

When we were in the hospital waiting room, we felt lonely and abandoned. Self-pity intensified. We finally dedicated ourselves to prayer. As we prayed God reminded us of friends that loved us, and this gave us the freedom to call them. Within hours faithful friends were by our sides. As he did with Elijah, God met us at our low point and brought us the fellowship and partnership we needed.

PROACTIVE RESOLVE #3

Spiritual health means accepting the aloneness that comes with ministry and pursuing the help, friendship, and fellowship we need to keep growing.

CHAPTER FOUR

THE HURDLE OF THE LEARNING PLATEAU: HAVE I STAGNATED?

"I'm taking a required course with Dr. Smith," Dave told me, "and it's a bore!"

"May I see your notes?" I asked.

The young seminarian was taking an introductory course taught by one of my former professors. Reading the notes, I flashed back to seminary days, and I laughed aloud as I came across the same outlines, the same quotations, and the same illustrations I had heard. But the thought struck me—his course content (including illustrations) had not changed in a dozen years. No wonder Dave found the course boring.

Thinking about Dr. Smith led me to criticism. How could a professor become so stagnant that one of his prime courses never changed? As I thought about Dr. Smith, the Holy Spirit broke through in a moment of convincing insight: And what about you? Aren't you giving the same lessons to freshmen that you've been giving for five years? And how about last month's retreat messages? Weren't they the same ones you gave in 1980?

My first instinct was self-defense. I offered all of my "Yes . . . buts," but I could not find peace. I had to come to realize that I was as guilty as Dr. Smith.

LIVING OFF OLD RESERVES

One of the hurdles to spiritual growth inherent in youth ministry is that we can live off of old reserves for a long time. The training we might have received in seminary, college, or through our church or parachurch group can last many years because youth work is repetitive. The students are constantly changing; even a student who comes to a high-school ministry regularly is gone in four years, and twenty-five percent of a group changes every year. While culture and themes change, the basic questions are fundamentally the same.

Thus, while I might have needed a new rock group or TV show to illustrate my point, my answers to basic teen issues were repetitive. Even my volunteers were turning over, so my training for them (after about two years) could be repeated. Parents and church leaders evaluated me by programs and student opinion, not by my learning. The senior pastor had a study. I had an office that stored volleyball equipment and the recently-donated popcorn maker. Even our youth worker's fellowship was more task-oriented. If we discussed a book, it was a pragmatic youth-ministry book. Few of us wrestled with theology, issues of social justice, or even sociology (except as it gave us great statistics to use in our next talk).

I was coming to grips with the fact that I might not be in danger of burning out, but I was definitely in danger of stagnating.

Youth ministry can create an environment that fosters a spiritual sloppiness in us. We need only four years (or less) worth of material, and we can survive forever. As a result, we can easily find ourselves in an environment where we are answering old questions about old topics with old answers. Dr. Robert Clinton of Fuller Theological Seminary calls this "the plateau barrier," a phenomenon that arrests a leader's development. He writes in *The Making of a Leader* that "leaders have a tendency to cease developing once they have some skills and ministry experience. They may be content to continue their ministry as is, without discerning a need to develop further."[1] Later in that book, Dr. Clinton makes this sobering observation: "Because of the rapid pace of change in our society, a leader who has plateaued is not stationary but is actually declining."[2]

> *Spiritual health requires us to recognize the*
> *plateau barrier inherent in the youth-ministry*
> *environment and to make changes that foster*
> *our growth.*

SHARPEN
THOSE BLADES

A man on a walk in the forest heard sounds of activity. He found another man furiously sawing at the base of a huge oak tree. The logger was about halfway through the trunk. The first man asked, "How long have you been at this?"

The logger replied, "About five hours."

"Why don't you take a break to stop and sharpen that saw?" asked the man.

"I cannot afford to do that," answered the logger. "I've got too much left to do."

If we want to operate effectively and efficiently with our gifts and resources, we must take time to sharpen our saws.

How do we know if we are at this plateau barrier? What are the signs of a dull spiritual blade? What will we look like when our spirits, like unexercised muscles, begin to atrophy?

Two veteran leaders offer some characteristics of stagnating spiritual or personal growth. Gail MacDonald, wife of pastor and author Gordon MacDonald, uses a similar analogy of staying sharp and offers an evaluative list of indications of an "unsharpened life" in her book *Keep Climbing*.[3] Mark Senter, Christian education professor, in the article "Five Stages in Your Ministry Development,"[4] adds other indicators of stagnation on the job. Their observations are combined below.

Language. "Poor mouth control" is one of MacDonald's indicators of an unsharpened life. If the mouth speaks out of what fills my heart (Matt. 12:36), and my heart is empty or bitter, the words will follow. Fresh water does not flow from stagnant pools. When sharp or cynical words flow freely from me or I am explosive with anger or pent-up hostility, it is a verbal demonstration to me of my spirit. I may be simply exhausted and need a rest. Or I may be revealing the degree of sanctification that remains to occur.

One experience in my early youth ministry illustrates the point well. I was in seminary, newly married, and trying to lead the high-school ministry. My candle was burning at both ends. A crisis occurred when students decided to "toilet paper" a home where our youth staff were having a planning retreat. When I saw it I became furious, yelling at the students, even rebuking a parent who had helped because he thought it was "an expression of their love."

It probably was an expression of their love, but I couldn't see it. My own spiritual condition erupted through my verbal comments.

Wrong goals. When I am running on spiritual empty, I begin to strive in the wrong direction for approval. I offer a sermon or a youth talk and measure its effectiveness based on how humorous I was or how good my illustrations were in contrast to last week's speaker. MacDonald writes, "people become my standard." Faulty goals such as success, comparing ourselves against others, and looking for approval become our focus.

Consistent growth often carries an accompanying sense of vision and purpose. In youth work spiritual stamina gives us the vision to stay patient and positive about students who seem incorrigible, families that seem irreparable, or demands that are unreasonable. In contrast, spiritual dryness often goes along with loss of vision. When a youth pastor told me that he was leaving a church ministry after four months because "they really didn't appreciate what I had to offer," I wondered if the church was the problem.

Whining or self-pity. MacDonald highlights self-pity as an indicator of an unsharpened blade because self-pity is often an outward expression of some perceived right that has been violated. When our rights become our focus, it indicates that we have regressed from consistent spiritual progress. Our focus has changed to ourselves and our needs.

One of the best ways to find out what is *really* in the hearts of youth workers is to listen to their conversations when they think no one else is listening. In the bathrooms of national conventions, I have listened while some youth workers have detailed to each other their respective lists of "apologies owed me." While I do not discount the fact that many youth workers are mistreated and underappreciated, whether it is by poor salaries, critical comments, or inferior working conditions, I still maintain that a strong commitment to consistent, personal spiritual growth helps keep us committed to the call to youth ministry.

When our focus becomes all of the ways that we are being under-supported, all of the things that we contribute that our churches never notice, or all of the better ways that *other* youth leaders get treated, we demonstrate the state of our spirits. If I detailed the ways I was treated in the earliest days of my youth ministry, I am sure you would agree that I might be justified for some hostility. But one day as I delineated my list of complaints to an older Christian, he responded, "But Paul, when are you going to let that history go?" He was pointing out to me that spiritual maturity and self-pity could not coexist.

Overinvestment in tasks. The church that Jesus addressed in Ephesus (Rev. 2) had plateaued spiritually. Their endurance, purity of doctrine, and deeds were unsurpassed, but they had lost their first love. They stood strong on tasks, but love was lacking. When we are drying up spiritually, we look for new ways to be challenged. As a result, people ministry (which is often intangible) gets sacrificed for tasks. We grow busier, more active, even overworked, in an effort to make up for the emptiness we feel within.

Several years ago a good friend noticed that I was doing more writing and extracurricular speaking. He knew me well enough to ask, "How much of your self-esteem is being hung on these outside responsibilities? Could you go for a year without writing?" My friend knew that my excessive, extracurricular involvement could be my way of running from spiritual dryness inside.

"As you struggle with the feelings of stagnation in the church," writes Mark Senter, "you tend to look for credibility and challenge outside—in hobbies, service clubs, or whatever. Unlike healthy outside interests, this is more of an escape."

Deceit. Living in a state of spiritual dullness in its progressed form leads to deceit. In this condition we become like the church in Laodicea. To them (and us) Jesus says, "I know your deeds; you have a reputation of being alive, but you are dead" (Rev. 3:1). The Laodiceans were living off of the reserves stored up during days of faithfulness, but now they were empty.

In youth ministry we know that we are living off the reputation of being alive (even when we are stagnating) when we find ourselves bluffing our students and our coworkers more and more. We advocate Bible memorization, but we seldom learn a new verse ourselves. We have personal Bible study and prayer times on retreats, mission teams, or camps to set a good example for the students, but we seldom crack the Bible or get on our knees at home. We exhort our students to witness, but we never find the time to reach out to our friends.

Senter writes, "You don't want to let on how you're feeling, and increasingly you mistrust other leaders." We find ourselves hiding our weaknesses, overexaggerating our strengths, and giving people the impression that we are much further down the growth road than we really are. The scariest part of inner deceit is that we can rationalize our behavior even to ourselves, a further indication of our spiritual stagnation. We become like the prideful emperor of the fable, trying to convince others that we are wonderfully dressed when in reality we are naked.

HAVE WE LOST THE WONDER?

The great Baptist preacher Vance Havner described the evangelist Gypsy Smith, who was an active preacher for seventy years. When asked the secret of his freshness and vigor, even into his old age, Smith replied, "I have never lost the wonder." Havner concludes his essay by telling the story of a passenger on a long train trip. When everyone was bored by the monotony of the trip, this one passenger kept exclaiming "wonderful" at the sight of the most average scenery. Finally he was asked by another traveler the reason for his conspicuous excitement. He answered, "Until a few days ago, I was a blind man. A great doctor has just given me my sight, and what is ordinary to you is 'out of this world' to me."[5]

Spiritual renewal means going back to Jesus, even in the face of our stagnation, and asking that our own eyes be reopened to the wonder of forgiveness, mercy, and a relationship with him.

PROACTIVE RESOLVE #4 _____

Spiritual health means identifying our own propensity to plateau and recommitting ourselves to disciplined growth.

CHAPTER FIVE

THE HURDLE OF LUST: AM I WAGING THE WAR WITHIN?

Moral failure. Sexual sin. Losing the battle with lust. Which story shall I tell?

Any communicator knows the need for good illustrations. Stories that make a point are valuable commodities, but often difficult to find. When I write, remembering, researching, or finding the best stories presents my greatest challenge. Yet when it comes to the matter of sexual failure or yielding to lust, my file is full. Of all the hurdles we are trying to clear in our endurance race, this is the one over which more runners seem to stumble.

I think of Dave whose leadership in ministry has been discredited because of his indiscreet joking with a teenage girl. Then there is Phil, a single youth worker whose ministry ended because he was caught peeking into the girls' shower room on the retreat. A careless touch of a young girl cost Ray credibility with the parents, and he eventually had to leave his church. Jan's confiding the story of a past affair to a fellow volunteer stirred rumors in her church to such an extent that she was forced to move to another location.

And these are not the most serious errors. Leaders joke about youth workers at conventions spending record amounts on hotels' pay-television movies, but who is laughing? An anonymous minister writes for *Leadership* magazine of his decades-long obsession with pornography.

It does not end there. There is Randy, the thirty-five-year-old youth pastor who left the ministry because of an affair with a teenager in the group; he now faces criminal charges. Or how about Brad, the youth leader who was discovered having sexual encounters with young boys in his youth group? As the tragic news became public, Brad could not come to grips with the shame that lay ahead, so he killed himself.

Lust. Pornography. Heterosexual and homosexual encounters. Affairs leading to devastated ministries and broken marriages. One wonders where it will stop. In the ongoing desire for spiritual health and growth, sexual temptation presents itself as a formidable foe.

> *Our own sinfulness plus the temptations*
> *associated with work in a sensual culture of*
> *maturing young people equals a recipe for*
> *sexual failure.*

THE ENVIRONMENTAL HAZARDS

Health-care experts alert us often these days to aspects of our lifestyle, atmosphere, and environment that can have long-term effects on our health. Whether it's inhalation of cigarette smoke, eating too much salt, or the radon levels in our homes, we are discovering more and more environmental hazards that we are supposed to avoid. But how can we, without moving to an isolated island or some mountain hideaway? Realistically, living in our world requires management of the environmental hazards we face. Few of us can afford to run from them totally.

In the same way, youth ministry presents us with sexual and moral challenges to our spiritual health. The following aspects of the youth-ministry environment create opportunities for sexual temptation.

Maturing young people. Most of the people we are working with are in the physiological stage known as puberty. Young men and women are growing from children to sexually (*not* mentally or emotionally) mature adults. In youth ministry we discuss self-esteem, hold seminars on sexuality, and refer to books like *Handling Your Hormones* (Jim Burns, Harvest House, 1986). We study books on the sexual maturing process so that we can help students. We find students (male or female) coming to us for advice or counsel. We sit through the Dobson films, interact with sex education at the public schools, and study the Bible to find out how to address kids in a sexually-saturated world.

Eventually, all of this sex talk has its effects. Who has not been tempted with wandering erotic thoughts about the young people we serve? Who has conquered the lust of the flesh that entices us at every turn? It's tough to keep our thoughts pure, especially as we seek to serve young women whose breasts are just developing and young men who spend time comparing the size of their penises. When we confiscate the pornographic literature from some students at youth camp, we find ourselves saving the books to thumb through, rationalizing that we need to see what the kids are looking at. The off-color jokes that frequently occur in the company of fellow youth workers remind me that I am not the only one who struggles here.

I suppose the best way to manage the stimulation that results is to rush home to our spouses. But what of the unmarried youth worker? Even being married, I find that my spouse gets tired of being greeted at the door by an overheated husband singing, "Well, I'm hot-blooded!"

Our own life situation. The fact that many youth leaders start in leadership in their early twenties presents another hazard. Now at age thirty-six and happily married, I can control my thoughts towards teenagers a little better simply by reminding myself that I am only a few years younger than many of their fathers. But when I was twenty-four, unmarried, and leading the youth group, it was never easy.

Even if we are married, the youth ministry schedule can invite problems. With the possible exception of the total husband/wife team ministry, many married youth leaders find themselves spending more time with students and volunteer staff than with their spouses or family. This situation invites unhealthy emotional dependencies and can foster emotional distance at home that can lead to moral failure.

Many of us in youth ministry are also parents of young children. Thus the overstimulated husband (allow me to assume a "typical ministry home" for a moment) comes home looking for affection and physical love. For the wife, who may be expecting a child or has spent the day caring for their two preschoolers, sexual love might be the furthest thing from her mind.

The media. All of us want to be on the cutting edge of youth ministry, so we desire to be up-to-date with what students are into. We stay attuned to developments in nearby high schools or trends across the country. But relevancy leads us into another arena that invites lust and destroys our spiritual health—the media. Videos, MTV, popular music, and contemporary movies are inseparable parts of the youth culture, and we do need some awareness of what students watch or listen to. But how much?

Do we need to watch and re-watch Madonna videos to know that she is provocative? How many R-rated movies are enough? Do we need to memorize the words of songs to illustrate their debauchery? Now that more of my ministry is with adults (so the desire to be relevant takes on different but equally tempting forms), I recognize the number of sexual images, word pictures, and adult themes that I have put into my mind that war against my soul (1 Pet. 2:11).

The ministry ego. Martin Luther said that "prayer, meditation, and temptation make a minister." He illustrated the multiple dimensions in the life of the ministry leader. Our desire for intimacy with God leads us to care for hurting people, but our sinfulness can skew this care into temptation and even failure. As we work with impressionable teenagers, we earnestly desire to care for and lead them. Yet in the course of things, their dependency and our care can become tainted or bent, like the midwestern senior pastor whose desire to help young men through puberty eventually degenerated to sexual abuse.

The young people may not be our only trouble. The volunteers who serve with us or single parents who need our support may come to us for pastoring. As our care-giving increases, interpersonal dynamics can intensify, leading to potential immorality.

SEXUAL BATTLEFIELDS

We could probably manage our environment fairly well, if that were our only enemy. The problems intensify, however, when we add a subjective dimension—our personal lustful and sinful natures. Earl Palmer, pastor of First Presbyterian Church in Berkeley, California, warns that "we have to talk about the very real temptations surrounding us, and not kid ourselves that we are somehow immune. Yet we can't blame everything on our environment. That's a cop-out. The environment has always been evil, and it is evil because there is evil in our hearts."[1]

How can we battle ourselves? The first step is identifying the battlefields. In my own experience and on the basis of my conversations with dozens of youth workers over the past few years, I think the problem manifests itself in three principal areas.

Fantasies and lustful thinking. To "take captive every thought to make it obedient to Christ" (1 Cor. 10:5) is a lofty goal for the purest of people, but for those of us who have allowed dirty stories or erotic images to permeate our thinking, the goal seems impossible. Harnessing my runaway mind is a gargantuan task. My ability to wander into lustful thinking seems to know no bounds. My mind can conjure up sexual images during prayer, while teaching, or in the midst of a baptismal service. Peter exhorts us to abstain from fleshly lusts that wage war against our souls (1 Pet. 2:11). Nowhere is the war more obvious than in this battle for our thoughts.

I once thought that marriage would cure me of lustful thoughts. As a single man I reasoned, When I get married and have an avenue of release for my passion, I will be all right. While getting married does offer some relief from the burning of passion (see 1 Cor. 7), it is not the panacea. The war continues, and our perverse minds can use healthy sexual relations in marriage as fuel for the flame of lust.

Pornography. I fled a music store the other day because the album covers were so erotic and sensuous that I was drifting into sinful thinking. In our society we must do a lot of fleeing. Pornography in pictorial or written form is everywhere. Ironically, this is the sin that many Christian leaders can enter into easiest. It feeds lust, but we rationalize that it is nowhere near as bad as adultery (evidently we forget Jesus' words in the Sermon on the Mount). We may never think of hiring a prostitute to satisfy our desires, but we purchase a book of pictures printed by someone who hired her for us. Pornography conjures up images of fantasy and feeds our minds, engulfing us in sin.

Masturbation. I was amazed when a veteran pastor bluntly explained a parishioner's divorce by saying, "Their marriage fell apart because the husband destroyed their sexual relationship by masturbation." In my naivete I had never thought that this could be an issue in a marriage.

In my years in youth ministry, I read many of the books on teenage sexuality. There seems to be a broad range of opinion on the issue of masturbation. Some say it is a normal part of growing up. Others refer to Romans 1, including masturbation as one stage in the degradation of humanity before God.

Very few books, however, address the issue as it might affect a marriage. Perhaps it is assumed that the problem just goes away, or maybe it is that everyone is too ashamed to talk about it. My conversations with fellow leaders tell me that the problem of masturbation does not go away. Fantasies and pornography, as well as television, movies, and a host of other sources, create sexual urges that even a sexually healthy marriage cannot fulfill. Masturbation, thought to be the natural release of these desires (isn't it amazing how we can fool ourselves with twisted logic?), serves to further the lust, which in turn pushes us towards fantasies and pornography.

LIVING IN
THE DARK

A restaurant near our home serves great food, but the place is always dark. On a bright summer day, we can walk into this restaurant to be served, and it will take ten minutes before we can read the menu. But over time, we get used to the dark. Our eyes adjust, and we become accustomed to the dimness. This is the problem with lust and sexual sin: We grow accustomed to the dark. The society we live in may be a dark contrast to the way of the Light, but over time, our spirits adjust; we become comfortable in the dimness. If we dedicate ourselves to spiritual health, we dare not get so used to the dark that we can no longer bear the light.

PROACTIVE RESOLVE #5 ⎯⎯⎯⎯⎯⎯⎯⎯⎯⎯⎯

Spiritual growth and health means engaging in the ongoing battle against lust and sexual temptation.

CHAPTER SIX

THE HURDLE OF BUSYNESS: CAN I FULFILL MULTIPLE EXPECTATIONS?

I was in San Francisco for the Youth Specialties National Youth Workers Convention when the now-famous October 1989 earthquake struck. The room shook and people jostled for the door. I followed suit without really knowing what was happening. No one in the seminar shouted "earthquake!" or any other warning. Most of them were Californians who knew what was happening.

When I returned home, local friends who had heard that I had been in San Francisco during the earthquake asked, "What was it like?" I struggled for analogies because it is not quite "like" anything. I tried to compare it with walking down the aisle of an airplane during turbulence or being tossed about on the deck of a ship in a storm. I finally arrived at this summary: When the earth is moving under your feet, you have an overwhelming feeling that *there is no place to hide*. In New England you can hide from a blizzard. If you heed the warnings, you can usually hide from a hurricane. But in an earthquake, there is no warning, no stability, no place to hide.

Youth leaders sometimes feel as though they live an earthquake life. A few years ago I started studying in the library until students found me there and started to arrange to run into me. On days off I tried not to answer my phone, but people from church found that I did this, so one lady called and let it ring for fifteen minutes until, like someone experiencing Chinese water torture, I couldn't stand the pressure any longer, and I answered it. After 10 p.m. my wife and I usually turn out the lights and go to bed, but that did not stop Phil when he needed to talk at 11:15 p.m.

Staying spiritually healthy in youth ministry is tough because it is full of many people with diverse expectations that cannot possibly be fulfilled in the time we have.

WHAT IS A YOUTH WORKER LIKE?

Several analogies provide the picture of the multiple demands and expectations thrust on the youth leader. Understanding these may help us comprehend more clearly why our spiritual "feeding" can be sacrificed in our efforts to fulfill expectations.

The youth worker is like an executive. We have full responsibility for our schedules, and there is usually no one hanging over our heads to watch how we manage our time. We only have the board to report to later, and at these meetings we find out if we have been investing our time wisely or not.

As the executive of First Church's youth ministry, Mark thought things were going along quite well. The youth discipleship groups were growing, and Sunday school was at an all-time high. After his first six months, Mark thought all was well. That is why he was so surprised when the chairman of the church board came by to tell him he had been fired. The board recognized his accomplishments, but they had decided what they really wanted was outreach to the inactive kids on the church rolls. Mark had not filled their uncommunicated expectations, so he would be removed. (Unlike an executive, however, Mark was given no severance pay.)

Most of us enter youth ministry without twenty years of experience behind us. When we get started, we are more like entry-level sales personnel who need someone over us to make sure that we are neither lazy nor burning ourselves out. Jay came as an intern to our youth ministry. He desperately wanted to succeed, so he over-prepared for everything. Finally, after he spent five hours preparing for a ten-minute devotional, I took him aside to teach him some youth-ministry survival skills, like balancing preparation time with the other demands of the ministry. He needed a supervisor who could help steer him away from patterns that could hinder his long-term effectiveness.

The youth worker is like a doctor. If we get a phone call, we are expected to be available. Like a doctor we are given care of patients who waited far too long before coming to see us. When we give them the prognosis, we incur their irrational wrath.

Mrs. Stetson called me in tears. Her son had come home drunk, and she was beside herself with grief. Could I see her and her son the next day (my day off)? I agreed to see them since it seemed that they were already in the spiritual emergency ward. As we talked that day, it was obvious that Kenny had gotten drunk in an effort to get his mother's attention. After forty-five minutes of discussion, I told his mother my observation. She flared up in anger. She had hoped I was going to lecture Kenny; she had not come to hear that she was part of the problem. The conversation ended abruptly, and they left.

Dealing with family emergencies is one of the youth minister's hardest jobs. Distraught parents bring in children who demonstrate the accumulated results of fifteen years of family dysfunction hoping that we can solve the problems in fifteen minutes.

The youth worker is like Yossarian in Catch-22. When someone calls and asks, "Are you busy?" I face a double jeopardy.

They could be calling expecting me to be their doctor. If I say yes, I'm busy, they might hang up, thinking that their problem is insignificant or that I'm unavailable to them. If I say no, I'm not busy, they could be one of the people who wonder, What exactly *do* you do? and they will respond, "I knew you wouldn't be busy."

The youth worker is like a circle. There is no apparent beginning or end to the work. A carpenter can start a table and finish it. A lawyer knows that even the most protracted case will eventually be over. But the youth minister graduates one class just to receive another. As soon as one need is met, five others emerge. The work is never finished.

The youth worker is like a pastor. He or she is not exactly a pastor; only the one who preaches is considered a *real* pastor. The youth leader preaches only on Youth Sunday and only assists in administering the Lord's Supper. But the youth leader must still know everything about the Bible and should behave "pastorally," especially at church functions.

All of us know the pain we feel inside when we are approached by parents who ask, "Are there any adults going with you on this trip?" We yearn for their full respect as adult, pastoral leaders, but for some reason, our commitment to youths diminishes our status in their eyes.

The youth worker is like a coach. There are lots of players in the big youth-ministry picture. The youth pastor is expected to get them all working together for the overall goal. Students, volunteers, parents, and other interested adults all make up the team, but getting these people with their diverse expectations to agree on the goal of the game presents a significant challenge. The youths desire a place to belong, volunteers desire to disciple, and parents want to keep their kids out of trouble. Others in the church might have a completely different agenda.

The youth worker is like God. Students need a youth leader who is omnipresent, especially as it pertains to them. Parents want a youth worker who is omnipotent with respect to family problems. Churches expect a youth pastor to be omniscient about everything from how to keep junior highers quiet during the services to how to keep students free from sickness on mission trips to the Amazon.

EVERYBODY WANTS A PIECE OF ME

As a teenager I envied rock stars whose adoring fans hung all over them. Now I am not so sure it would be as much fun as I thought. The pressures of having numbers of people hanging their needs and expectations on us can become intolerable if we do not find some way to manage it. Gail MacDonald writes that "unless there is a strong sense of purpose lurking somewhere within us, we can expect our lives either to bang about like a ball in a pinball machine or to come under the control of those who are more than glad to create purposes for us."[1]

Consider the following people whose expectations might cause us to bang about or whose desire to control pulls at our energy and time.

Ourselves. Our inflated expectations of ourselves can cause some of the greatest pressures on us, especially internally.

Family. Our spouses or children provide a welcome pull on us, but we still may live under the constant fear that we are disappointments to our spouses and poor parents to our children because we are away from them so much.

Students in our group. They expect us to be their pastor, their friend, their advocate, their program planner, and their surrogate parent. We live under the pressure that even if one student feels loved, another might feel ignored.

Parents of students. Their expectations range from baby-sitter to miracle worker. If we work in the church, parents may expect us to produce missionaries. If we work in the para-church (with students from nonchurchgoing families), parents may expect a great program with a light seasoning of God or morality.

Our volunteers. Some volunteers want our full attention; they may have entered the youth ministry to be discipled by us. Others want to be left alone; they may even wonder why we get paid when they are doing all the work.

Our superiors. In the church this could be elders, deacons, presbyters, or youth council (although all church members may think themselves our bosses). They may expect the biggest and best program in town. In the parachurch ministry, this would be our local board, who may or may not communicate clearly what they expect.

The broader Christian community. Church parishioners who are not related to youth work, the ministerial association, or even a youth worker's fellowship group can place pressure on us in one way or another—help with this church function, attend that luncheon, support this combined event.

The community at large. In some settings the youth leader is expected to help out in school functions, work closely with the local police, and attend community activities.

The expectations of these groups are by no means all negative. Who does not love a four-year-old tugging at her hand saying, "Mommy, stay home; no more meetings"? But the multiple expectations build up, and we find ourselves running in a dozen different directions. Personal or ministry goals are sacrificed to the tyranny of the urgent, and in the face of it all, spiritual growth slows down or grinds to a halt.

HURRY SICKNESS

I recently read an article in an airline magazine that focused on the "disease" they called "hurry sickness." Hurry sickness, the psychologist-author wrote, is when we hurry through every activity of the day just to get to the next activity. Although written for corporate executives, I could see myself fit his description. The symptoms included eating food too fast, being short-tempered in talking to those we love most, and expressing aggression in our driving habits.

Youth work can foster hurry sickness, and as someone said, "If the Devil can't make you bad, he'll make you busy." Identifying the multiple expectations and realistic limits of our time and our lives is the first step towards averting hurry sickness in our spiritual growth.

PROACTIVE RESOLVE #6 _____

Spiritual health and growth require an offensive perspective on our time (using it to achieve balanced purposes) and a realistic idea of our limited abilities to fulfill the expectations of others.

SECTION TWO

WORKING OUT FOR SPIRITUAL GROWTH

I recently had the frightening experience of finding that my blood pressure was unusually high. Over the days that followed, I monitored my pressure twice a day. As the days went by and the problem continued, I found myself leaning towards rationalizations. I tried to skew the data to make it seem like I was getting better. I desired to hide the results from my wife in an effort to give the impression that the problem had ceased. But it did not just go away. No matter how much I rationalized, the blood pressure readings did not lie. I had a problem that I needed to deal with, and I could not until I stopped bluffing myself. Restoration of health would not come until I was honest.

Many of us experience a parallel situation with our spiritual condition. Something draws our attention to the spiritual need in our lives. Perhaps a book, a speaker, a day to think, or an encounter with a sinful failure that we never thought possible highlights a gap in our spiritual health. Over the days that follow, we monitor our progress and look optimistically for signs that the problem is going away. If it lingers we face a choice: Will we go the route of rationalization, or will we allow an honest confrontation of our need? Both the restoration of and maintenance of our spiritual health require honesty.

ESSENTIALS IN THE SPIRITUAL EXERCISE

As we look at the exercises in the next chapters, what essential truths about ourselves will provide a foundation on which to build?

First, coming face to face with God's expectations and priorities for us versus our own. We may take a step back and realize that what we are trying to become is out of step with what God has called us to be. Somewhere along life's highway we took the wrong exit ramp, and we need to get back on the road God wants for us. For some, evaluating God's priorities will convince us that we are involved with more than God intended. For reasons ranging from insecurity to the so-called Messiah complex, many of us have assumed more responsibility than God assigns. An honest evaluation may call us to let go of some areas of leadership.

Second, recommitting ourselves to the concept that growth is a process, not a one-time event. No one has truly "ordered their private world."[1] We face ourselves honestly and realize that while we can be consistent in striving to be like Christ, we seem to miss it as much as we hit it.

Finally, finding that in Christ there is freedom. A few of us may find the exercises that follow to be a call to intensified disciplines of prayer, Scripture study, and meditation. Others may decide to go away for two days rest. Some of us may take up a book and others may pursue silence. Strength for some will come from peer relationships while others seek a mentor. As the president of Eastern College, Dr. Roberta Hestenes, has pointed out, "people are on different spiritual journeys and have different needs and circumstances and temperaments. Therefore, not everyone should do the same spiritual disciplines in the same ways. We want to respect that God-given diversity."[2]

All of us can agree that we need to grow. The chapters that follow provide catalysts in that process.

CHAPTER SEVEN

FORGIVENESS: LEARNING TO LET GO OF FAILURE

After a vacation I enjoy taking our film to the processor so that a few days later we can enjoy the pictures that remind us of the time away. That is, I *used* to enjoy this . . . until the most recent batch of photos came back. We had spent a week on the beach in our bathing suits. I did not like what I saw. The photos of me with my shirt off visibly reminded me of what I was becoming. The overlapping belly (and I had even remembered to suck in my gut when Christie was taking the picture!), the fat rolls, and my generally poor physical condition was vividly portrayed on film. I vowed to hide the camera before the next vacation.

Few of us enjoy personal expose, especially if it contains a revelation of self that we usually keep hidden from others or ourselves. But looking into the Scriptures, coming to terms with the standards of Christ-likeness, and pursuing spiritual growth provides a set of photos that reveal our innermost state. Spiritual health (like physical fitness) starts when we acknowledge our present status. Until I acknowledge that the vacation photos depict the real me and are not some result of a wide-angle lens, I cannot begin to restore physical fitness. Until we learn to agree with God about our failures and receive the forgiving love of Jesus Christ, we are stunting our growth. When we find, however, that no failure is too great for him, we are free to grow.

CONFESSION:
THE STARTING POINT

I will assume that anyone who is reading a book on feeding our forgotten souls is probably already sensitized to the multiple flaws in our spiritual performance. Some of you may be reading because you feel that secret sins in the past or present disqualify you from continuing as a leader of others, yet you yearn to know God's grace. Others of you may simply sense that your spiritual vitality is waning. I doubt if any of us feel smug and self-satisfied as to spiritual health.

Whatever our personal state, we all need to get on the growth track by confession. Confession, the acknowledgement of inner and outward expressions of rebellion against God's standards, establishes the foundation to receive in a fresh way Jesus' forgiveness and love and (in the best-case scenario) the forgiveness and love of his people. Confession is a journey inward. Sometimes it is helpful to read a psalm of confession (Psalms 32 and 51 have been the most helpful to me) to trigger our thoughts and remind us of the ways we have blown it before God. Confession means bowing humbly before Jesus and agreeing aloud with the following confession found in the *Book of Common Prayer*. (I recommend pausing to meditate after every major phrase.)

> Almighty and most merciful Father; we have erred, and strayed from Thy ways like lost sheep. We have followed too much the devices and desires of our own hearts. We have offended against thy holy laws. We have left undone those things which we ought to have done; and we have done those things which we ought not to have done; and *there is no health in us* [emphasis mine]. But thou, O Lord, have mercy upon us, miserable offenders. Spare thou those, O God, who confess their faults. Restore thou those who are penitent; according to thy promises

declared unto mankind in Christ Jesus our Lord. And grant, O most merciful Father, for his sake; that we may hereafter live a godly, righteous, and sober life, to the glory of thy holy name. Amen.[1]

Acknowledging that we are not spiritually healthy is not a popular idea in a culture obsessed with personal potential and self-actualization. Most of us would like to find *something* that we could present before God as a defense of our value (like the Pharisee in Luke 18), but true confession is putting ourselves totally at God's mercy (like the sinner in Luke 18). Until we can confess before God that we have within ourselves the capacity for evil through and through, we will not fully understand his grace.

RECEIVING FORGIVENESS

I find it easier to confess sins than to receive forgiveness. Depending somewhat on personality and how love and forgiveness were exemplified in our homes, each of us responds differently to forgiveness. Although I was not raised as a Roman Catholic, penance is a concept I can easily understand. For a variety of reasons, I find it difficult to believe that anyone (even God) could love me and forgive me as I am. Earning forgiveness or love, doing good to outweigh bad, and always working to win approval comes naturally to me. When I fail my wife, I apologize profusely and then try to make up to her with love notes, presents, or volunteering to do some chore around the house. My background has made it difficult for me to understand that she has forgiven me and loves me just the way I am.

Others might receive forgiveness without reservation. Perhaps a parent communicated an unconditional love that made it easier to fail and rebound. Those lucky ones often experience great freedom in their relationships with God, but even those folks will eventually encounter others who do not forgive so freely.

The conclusive teaching of the Scriptures is that somehow—by grace, mercy, and love—God is willing to take us in in spite of our sins. God has caused our sins to fall on Jesus, and we can be forgiven (see Isa. 53:6; 2 Cor. 5:21). To others we might say, If you really knew me, you wouldn't like me, but to us God says, I know you completely, and I love you as you are.

All of us desperately need a daily bath in God's forgiveness so that we can stay on the growing edge in our relationship to him. But we also need to receive the grace and forgiveness of Christ so that we can communicate forgiveness to those we serve. A young man wrote to me, "I am entangled in sexual sin, but I cannot talk about it with my pastor or youth worker. If I told them, it would sever our relationship." I never found out if the young man was correct in his evaluation of those relationships, but I wrote back, "If your pastor and youth worker truly come to grips with their own sinfulness and God's forgiveness, nothing you can tell them will sever their love for you." I wrote with the assumption that they had received, and therefore could help another find, forgiveness.

The young man's letter highlights a need that many of us have for a confessor. Liturgical traditions have long affirmed the need for a fellow human being with whom we can talk freely about our sins and who personifies (by their scriptural pronouncement of forgiveness in Jesus Christ) the love and forgiveness of God. When sins are weighing us down, a confessor can be not only the voice of God's forgiveness, but also the prescriber of remedial action to help us break free of the sin. In his book *Rebuilding Your Broken World* (Oliver Nelson, 1988), my former pastor Gordon MacDonald refers to four men (he calls them his "angels") who served both as confessors and prescribers and helped him experience the grace of Christ and rebound from sin.

Our sins act like unwanted anchors, weighing us down when we would rather be free to sail. Whether we are bound by lust or deceit, busyness or gossip, we need help. A confessor (or, as I prefer to call them, an accountability partner) can help us find release from the weight.

GETTING BACK UP

One of my sermons last summer was a bomb. I knew it. The people who heard me knew it. I left the church that night feeling defeated and sorry for myself. I vowed in the emotion of the moment that I would never preach again. God might be able to use me in some other way, but my speaking days were over. Then he brought to mind a verse that has helped me understand forgiveness and restoration: "For though a righteous man falls seven times, he rises again" (Prov. 24:16). Rebounding from failure is illustrated throughout the Scriptures by King David, Peter, Mary Magdalene, and others, but this succinct verse sums it all up. Righteousness, or staying in a healthy relationship with God, involves "falling seven times" (a Hebrew saying that probably means falling repeatedly). Even those who most desire to follow Christ fall.

What determines our growth is our response to falling—will we rise again? Will we get back up? Will we sit in the mud, wallow in self-pity, and lament our wickedness? Or will we rise up, go to Jesus to confess our sins, and receive his forgiveness so that we can get back on track? The decision we make determines a life of spiritual frustration versus a life of growth.

Pastor Donald McCullough in his book *Waking From the American Dream* writes of the need we all have to fail forward. "What will we do with failure? We have a choice. Either we can withdraw, or we can learn the discipline of failing forward."[2] The principle of Proverbs 24:16 is the principle of failing forward: When we fall, let us learn from our errors, get back up by God's power, and move ahead!

GIVING FORGIVENESS

Experiencing God's forgiveness comes with difficulty for some of us, but we can gradually learn as we meditate on the Cross of Christ and his love for us. Communicating God's forgiveness may come easy to us, especially as we tell of Jesus' love to young, malleable people who may be hearing about it for the first time. Granting forgiveness, however, is more difficult.

As a young Christian, I could never understand how Christians could hold grudges against each other. I heard of two brothers who had not spoken to each other in six years, and I wondered, Where is the love of Jesus? As I have grown older, however, I have learned how grudges are formed. People, even our Christian family, can cause us great personal pain. Unkind words cut to the core of our character, especially if they come from our brothers or sisters in Christ. When we start dealing with people who have sinned directly against us, and who— more often than not—have never asked our forgiveness, we find out whether the love of Jesus is really at work in us.

A youth worker came to me emotionally broken about the issue of granting forgiveness. As he told me of the abusive home in which he was raised, I vowed never to treat lightly the challenge that some face when forgiving those who have hurt them. This man did not want to carry the scars of his past with him for the rest of his life, but he was trying desperately to forgive them their sins. Forgiving those who have caused us great pain is itself painful.

Kim came to talk with me about the hostile treatment she had received from her church. We had met a year earlier and had discussed some legitimate complaints she had about her salary, the poor communication, the way her family was hurt, and the lack of support she received from the pastor. When we met a second time, it seemed that many things had improved at her church, but as we talked it became evident that the pain of the past was *very* close to the surface. She began to vent her hurt again, citing all of the events of a year before. After listening, I finally asked the words that another had spoken to me: "When are you going to let that history go? When are you going to pronounce your church, your pastor, and the board forgiven, even if they never ask?"

As God chose to love us "while we were still sinners" (Rom. 5:8), we need to choose to forgive others even when the hurt is still there. Hanging on, bearing a load of grudges, and refusing to release those that have hurt us in the past usually anchors us down and keeps us from growing. Let it go.

A friend shared with me a perspective that helped her let go of someone who had sinned against her. She said, "As long as I thought about the hurt caused, I thought of that person as an enemy, one who endangered me and caused me pain. When I focused on Jesus, I realized that this person was a spiritual captive to sin who needed to be released. I found the grace to forgive by distinguishing a captive from an enemy."

TAKING
STOCK

In the exercise of forgiveness, consider several questions to assist in positive spiritual growth:

- Are there sins in my life I have been tolerating by rationalizing that my good deeds are outweighing my bad? Am I willing to look at myself honestly?
- Is there some secret sin that is eating me away internally? If so, will I . . .
  — bring it to God?

— allow him to forgive me?
— forgive myself and get back up?
— confess it to a friend to find assistance in understanding God's love and forgiveness?
— ask someone for help to find restoration and grace?
- Is there someone I need to seek out to ask forgiveness?
- Is there someone I need to let go by pronouncing him or her forgiven in my heart, even if there has never been an apology?

HEALTHY PAIN

Looking at ourselves honestly is a painful process. I hate to see pictures that remind me of being overweight and in poor condition. But I need to see the photos so that I can remedy the situation. Looking at a spiritual photo of ourselves can be equally painful, but understanding and exercising the forgiveness of God in our lives emanates outward from an understanding of God's love toward us. When we understand that he loves us as we are, we are freed to grow towards what he desires us to be.

J.I. Packer concludes his powerful chapter on "The Love of God" (*Knowing God*, InterVarsity, 1973) with other questions of self-evaluation. While not directly related to granting forgiveness, they remind us of the foundation of forgiveness—God's love toward us. If God indeed is showing his love towards us,

- Why do I grumble and show discontent and resentment at the circumstances in which God has placed me?
- Why am I distrustful, fearful, or depressed?
- Why do I allow myself to grow cool, formal, and half-hearted in the service of the God who loves me so?
- Why do I allow my loyalties to be divided, so that God has not all my heart?[3]

CHAPTER EIGHT

SPIRITUAL DISCIPLINES: SPIRITUAL GROWTH DOES NOT JUST HAPPEN

"Why do you come to Sister Shar'ns revival meetings?" the charlatan Elmer Gantry asked the custodian cleaning up the tent.

"Well," explained the stogie-smoking old man, "Sister Shar'n comes to town and I gets saved, but after she leaves, I goes back to getting drunk, so I come back to hear her so's I can get saved again."

The custodian's reply illustrates the spiritual roller coaster that we all ride. We get revived, we fall, then need to get revived again. It is a cycle we are all too familiar with.

Tim Conder, the high-school leader at Grace Chapel, was reviewing summer mission-team application forms with me. He came to John's and remarked, "Here's one from our mission-trip Christian," a young man who had a pattern of getting serious about his faith after a rowdy year, just in time to go on one of the cross-cultural mission teams. Tim observed that John was no different than Elmer Gantry's custodian, only in John's case, the mission trip was his annual revival, not a series of tent meetings.

How can we avoid a similar cycle of fluctuation? Is there a way to sustain positive spiritual growth without the ups and downs we are so accustomed to?

Spiritual disciplines, both external and internal, can build our spiritual muscle and help us grow with consistency.

EXTERNAL DISCIPLINES

Several years ago runner and author Jim Fixx, who had taught and motivated thousands of others to take up jogging, dropped dead of a heart attack. His external frame was in great shape, but there were short circuits internally.

King David wrote of his praises to God every day, often three times a day, but his external spiritual disciplines of prayer or praise could not hide his wickedness, demonstrated by committing adultery with Bathsheba, which led to deceit and murder.

As we consider the externals of Christian discipline (Scripture memory, Bible study, prayer time, for example), we should never mistake them for ends in themselves or as some kind of insurance policy against sin. Fixx illustrates physically and King David illustrates spiritually that externals are not enough. But external disciplines do help us get on the right track. We cannot put false trust in them, but we should grow through them. What we are really after is growth in our characters, to be changed to look more and more like Jesus, and the externals provide the environment for this growth. Things that we can do are God-given avenues to assist us in our pilgrimage of growth. While they are not guarantees of internal character change, they stimulate us to grow in ways that God can use to change us from within.

Dozens of books are available on various spiritual disciplines designed to encourage growth. Richard Foster's *Celebration of Discipline* (Harper & Row, 1978) is worth reading at least once every few years. Dallas Willard's new book, *The Spirit of the Disciplines* (Harper & Row, 1988), is a little more tedious, but it does offer insights on how God changes lives through the spiritual disciplines, addressing such topics as prayer, fasting, and the vows of poverty.

Rather than elaborate on special disciplines that appeal to the broader Christian community, let's focus on three that are very basic and that are usually challenge enough for the over-taxed youth leader.

Scripture reading. Here is a question almost guaranteed to induce awkwardness at a youth leaders' gathering: What are you reading in the Bible lately? When I have tried it out, a few have had fresh answers, but others seem to be digging way back in time to respond. A few refer to what the youth group is studying, while others shrink away from answering. Even when everybody answers positively, asking, What's the last verse you have memorized? often brings a hush over the group.

The awkwardness is not because we do not want to be in Scripture. It is just that something else always seems to get in the way. The tyranny of the urgent, lack of time, or ministry needs (when we are studying for Bible studies but not reading it for ourselves) pushes the Bible out of our lives. In spite of our own problems reading the Bible daily, we would all respond to a student who asked, "How can I grow in my relationship with God?" by encouraging him or her to read the Bible.

Charles Spurgeon exhorted his ministry students to "eat into the very soul of the Bible until, at last, you come to talk in scriptural language, and your spirit is flavored with the words of the Lord, so that your blood is Bibline and the very essence of the Bible flows from you."[1] Reading this makes me feel guilty because I realize how far I am from such a state.

Whether we recognize it or not, whether we have drifted from it or not, the Bible is still our primary tool for understanding God's will and for becoming the person he wants us to become. The problem is that after one or two times through the Bible, we begin to focus our attention elsewhere. We read books about the Bible, then wander into books about biblical themes, and eventually we may find ourselves spending all of our reading time in literature about the Christian life and ministry without reading the source book.

All of this extra-biblical reading can be useful, but not if we neglect the Scriptures in the process. As youth leaders we are called by God to fulfill pastoral functions toward the people in our care. Like the apostles, our first concern should be "prayer and the ministry of the Word" (Acts 6:4). Yet how can we minister the Word to others if we are neglecting it ourselves? John R. Stott, internationally known writer and speaker, writes that "the Scripture comes alive to the congregation [in our case, to the youth group or youth-leadership team] only if it has come alive to the preacher first."[2]

In recovering personal reading and study of the Bible as part of our spiritual growth, consider these ideas that may help in our recovery—especially if we find ourselves in a spiritual rut:

- Get a new version of the Bible, or at least a new copy. Reading past underlining or notes in the margins seldom edifies as much as the Scriptures afresh.
- Have a plan. Reading randomly across the pages usually directs us to favorite passages at the expense of the more difficult ones. A plan to read through the Bible introduces us to the whole counsel of God.
- Put "read the Bible" as part of the weekly or daily schedule, and honor the time as if it were an appointment.
- Do a personal study. Reading offensively (for our own growth) usually affects us more than reading defensively (reading in preparation for a lesson).
- Get a one-year Bible or a one-year New Testament. I did this a year ago, and it helped me out of the doldrums of my Bible reading and through the entire New Testament.

Personal Worship. When I first became a Christian, enthusiasm and desire, combined with a flexible student schedule, enabled me to go for weeks, even months without missing a period of personal worship every day. Then I entered ministry. I got married. The demands of the ministry and the desire to spend free moments with my wife squeezed out personal worship time. Now I consider it a successful week if I can spend quality time in personal worship three or four times a week. Some may call this compromise or lack of effort. I call it reality.

In Luke 10, the images of Mary versus Martha in Jesus' presence illustrate the tension of our age. While we know that we should sit quietly at Jesus' feet (imitating Mary), we act more like Martha, scurrying about in our overcommitted efforts to serve (and wondering why others are not as committed as we are).

Busyness is the enemy of quietness, yet quietness is mandatory for worship. Basic Christian growth presumes that we are spending time in the presence of God. The Bible seems to imply that the more time we spend in Jesus' presence, the more we will begin to look like him (see Acts 4:13; 1 John 3:2). We all believe it, but do we practice doing it?

Do the following responses sound familiar?

- "Well, I tried renewing my personal worship time. Since we have little children, I moved it to the evenings, but on the days I do try, I keep falling asleep."
- "I sit down to read, get quiet, and pray, but I cannot seem to stay focused."
- "Every time I start, I begin thinking about the youth group. I end up writing out next week's lesson."
- "I'm already so worn out, I'm afraid that if I get quiet with God, he'll show me some new area of my life that needs work, and I'll snap."

The excuses abound, and they all may be true. So what can we do? Even if we believe that we *should* spend time in personal worship, what do we do when it seems impossible?

My greatest word of encouragement is **Don't give up!** Granted, we may not be getting the kind of worship time with the Lord that we would like, but we don't quit just because of the frustrations. Apply again the Proverbs 24:16 principle: Get back up. Woody Allen humorously stated, "Eighty percent of life is showing up." We often need to apply the same principle to personal worship time: Even when we feel rushed, we can take the time (even if it's five minutes) to present ourselves to Jesus. If it is not enough, it is still better than nothing.

Service. One of the basic disciplines of Christian growth is an outward expression of love for Christ through service. A youth worker might respond, "My whole life is service; how much more can I give?" Many youth leaders find themselves hard-pressed to give more than they are currently giving. As a result, I would like to encourage not more service but *more purpose* in our serving. In other words, rather than serving that moody junior higher or counseling that indecisive teenager "because it's my job," take an occasional step back to pray and remember that by serving we are actively seeking to imitate the Lord Jesus Christ.

Tony Campolo encourages youth leaders across the country to pursue service; because in serving the poor, the disadvantaged, and the hurting, we—in the spirit of Jesus' teaching in Matthew 25—are serving Jesus himself. Campolo's point illustrates that directed serving—that is, service offered with a distinct spiritual focus—changes our attitudes.

Recently after an exhausting day of ministry, I attended an evening service where God's spirit seemed to be mightily at work. At the close the service leader asked me to assist in counseling any who came forward for prayer. I was so tired that (I confess) I secretly hoped no one would come, so that I could go home and go to bed.

People started to come, and I was called into action. I asked God to help me to see people with his compassion, and I prayed along the lines of Philippians 4:13—"I can love these people through Christ who strengthens me." People came forward for prayer and counsel for over an hour, and in each case, God granted me the grace to listen, empathize, and pray with people in need. I still went home exhausted, but taking the brief moment to pray at the beginning made the difference in my growth through purposeful serving.

INTERNAL DISCIPLINES: MEASURING MERCURY

Measuring our growth through the external contributors to spiritual health is easier than trying to quantify internal matters like Christ-like character or Godly compassion. I can tell you how much of the Bible I am reading or how often I stop for personal worship, but how do I measure kindness? Nevertheless, we need to ask questions about matters of character, because fulfilling external disciplines (reading the Bible, personal worship time, and service) can become mundane and empty if they are not penetrating our spirits.

What does it mean to look Christ-like? Measuring our growth in character cannot be quantified in pounds or pages, but we can take time for self-evaluation that can at least point us to areas in our lives we can be praying about. Consider the following five options. Any one of these could challenge our character development for a year or more.

Measure ourselves against Jesus' growth patterns in Luke 2:52. Am I growing . . .

- In wisdom (intellectually: Is my mind being stretched?)
- In stature (physically: Am I taking care of my body?)
- In favor with God (spiritually: Am I obeying him in the things he has *already* revealed?)
- In favor with man (socially: Am I developing friendships to stir my growth?)

Measure ourselves against the fruit of the Spirit listed in Galatians 5:22. Go through each characteristic, and pray for God's wisdom to know where growth is needed.

- Love: Am I reaching out to parents or students that I cannot love without Jesus' help?
- Joy: Do I know how to rejoice, even when circumstances are tough?
- Peace: How do I react when circumstances are obviously out of my control?
- Kindness: Do my spouse, children, or others I live with think I am kind?
- Goodness: Do I want to do good as much as I want to be successful?
- Faithfulness: Where do I need help in perseverance?
- Gentleness: Am I emulating Jesus by inviting broken people into my presence?
- Self-control: Do I live by discipline or by the emotion of the moment?

Measure ourselves against Micah 6:8 (or the parallel verse in Deut. 10:12). Am I loving mercy, doing justice, and walking humbly with God? One friend of mine sets spiritual goals each year according to this verse. He established one or two things to do to (a) demonstrate mercy to broken people, (b) fight for justice for exploited people, and (c) challenge himself in his growth with God. To make this possible in youth-ministry leadership, one could involve the youth group in applying the verse.

Do a character evaluation with a trusted friend who will affirm and confront us on personal growth and where we need work.

Keep a spiritual-growth journal. After a year, look over the entries to discover patterns of discernible growth or obvious vacancies. Are we growing more compassionate in our references to others? Do our entries reflect peace in the face of crises? Is there notable growth in our brokenness over sin and our desire for holiness?

PLANNING FOR SPONTANEITY

How much does spiritual growth depend on our efforts, and how much does it just happen? Eugene Peterson, pastor and author, addresses this question in his article, "Growth: An Act of the Will?"[3] In it he shows how our efforts and God's efforts work hand in hand in spiritual growth, even if we do not always understand how.

We do not always understand how it happens, but we do know that if we evaluate our characters according to the standards of God *and* discipline our lives according to his Word, worship, and service, growth is a predictable result. Consistent growth in the spiritual disciplines will then become an exercise that helps us get *and stay* in good spiritual condition.

Call for fast service:
(619) 440-2333

BUSINESS REPLY MAIL
FIRST CLASS   PERMIT NO. 16   EL CAJON, CA

POSTAGE WILL BE PAID BY ADDRESSEE

YOUTH SPECIALTIES
1224 Greenfield Dr.
El Cajon, CA 92021-9989

II.I.....I.IIII.....I.I...IIII.I.I.I..I.I.I.....III

Call for fast service:
(619) 440-2333

NO POSTAGE
NECESSARY
IF MAILED
IN THE
UNITED STATES

BUSINESS REPLY MAIL
FIRST CLASS   PERMIT NO. 16   EL CAJON, CA

POSTAGE WILL BE PAID BY ADDRESSEE

YOUTH SPECIALTIES
1224 Greenfield Dr.
El Cajon, CA 92021-9989

II.I.....I.IIII.....I.I...IIII.I.I.I..I.I.I.....III

The People Who Brought You This Book...

Invite you to discover MORE valuable youth ministry resources.

Youth Specialties offers an assortment of books, publications, tapes and events, all designed to encourage and train youth workers and their kids. Just check what you're interested in below and return this card, and we'll send you FREE information on our products and services.

Please send me FREE information I've checked below:

☐ The Complete Youth Specialties Catalog and information on upcoming Youth Specialties events.

Name _____

Address _____

City _____ State _____ Zip _____

Phone Number ( ) _____

The People Who Brought You This Book...

Invite you to discover MORE valuable youth ministry resources.

Youth Specialties offers an assortment of books, publications, tapes and events, all designed to encourage and train youth workers and their kids. Just check what you're interested in below and return this card, and we'll send you FREE information on our products and services.

Please send me FREE information I've checked below:

☐ The Complete Youth Specialties Catalog and information on upcoming Youth Specialties events.

Name _____

Address _____

City _____ State _____ Zip _____

Phone Number ( ) _____

CHAPTER NINE
LEARNING: BREAKING OUT OF STAGNATION

Most professional sports teams offer some variation of the old-timers game each year. At this event players from the past reemerge, stuff themselves into the old uniform, and compete against each other to entertain the crowd. The old-timers game often embarrasses as much as it entertains. Agile superstars of the past now seem uncoordinated and slow. Physiques provide only a vague shadow of the sinewy bodies of years before. The game vividly illustrates that the athletes have stagnated; age and life situations have caused them to lose the edge.

Ongoing ministry can act in the same way. Repetitive ministry, consistent outpouring of our lives, and the stagnation alluded to in Chapter Four can set in, causing us to lose our edge. It may not be as demonstrable as the athletes' performance at the old-timers game, but we know it.

The remedy is another exercise, a discipline. If we are going to stay in shape and grow spiritually, we need to continue learning. The discipline of learning determines the difference between stagnation and "a mind alive."[1]

Jesus calls us to discipleship, a term derived from the verb "to learn" in the Greek language. If we are weak and burdened by life's cares, he invites us to come to him, lay our burdens on him, and learn from him (Matt. 11:28-30). In following Jesus we shall find rest for our souls.

In the previous chapter, I alluded to the difference between learning defensively versus learning offensively. In the former, our growth might only include reading and studying so that we can prepare for the next Bible study, the next Sunday-school lesson, the upcoming retreat talks. We are disciplining ourselves to grow even if we do not immediately need to. The question of this chapter is this: Are we learning offensively? Our ultimate goal is growing to be more like Jesus, but what does he look like? Evaluating our growth according to the four realms of Luke 2:52, for example, helps us identify where we need to start. But let's go further.

COMMITTING OURSELVES TO LEARN

In *The Making of a Leader*, author Robert Clinton of Fuller Seminary challenges every leader to be a learner.

> One of the striking characteristics seen in effective leaders is their desire to learn. They learn from all kinds of sources. They learn from Scripture. They are pressed by their situation to see new truth in the Scriptures and in the situations themselves. They learn about their own uniqueness. They build on the natural abilities they have. They acquire skills needed by the challenges of the situations they face. They learn to use their spiritual gifts ... *Effective leaders, at all levels of leadership, maintain a learning posture through life.*[2]

As youth leaders we look at that statement in the same way I watch Michael Jordan play basketball or Luciano Pavarotti sing. It is a lofty goal to aim for, but it is entirely out of my personal reach. A learning posture through life sounds impossible because I am trying to make it through the weekend.

We need to start where we are. To the best of our abilities, we need to take an offensive approach with our time, using it to achieve balance. So how can the youth leader modify his or her life to start growing as a learner?

Reading. A seminar at a pastor's conference was titled, "Send Us a Pastor Who Reads." Congregations may struggle to support the pastor while he studies, so it is no wonder that their expectations of us militate against our reading as youth leaders. Even though we may be encouraged to be resident youth experts, finding time to read presents a serious challenge.

So what can we do? First, we can start with the defensive reading mentioned before. The Scriptures, books related to teen culture, and even a new youth-ministry book might be a start. Our job enables us to read things that no one else might be reading about adolescent development, parent/teen relationships, and the high-school world. If we look at this reading as a growth opportunity, we can learn about the people we serve, both young people and adults, in new ways. In reading about adolescent development, I have learned about myself, understanding more deeply how the experiences of my youth have made me who I am today.

Second, we can set some reading goals for relaxation as well as intellectual growth not directly related to youth ministry. One youth minister reads Tom Clancy novels for recreation. Another studies such spiritual classics as Augustine's *City of God* and St. John of the Cross's *Dark Night of the Soul*. Reading for spiritual growth expands our minds as well as our souls. Earl Palmer writes, "As well as being physically well and spiritually committed, we need to be intellectually growing if we are to be effective Christians in the world."[3]

Finally, we can wake up to the world around us. When I desire to understand more about people's needs, I go to the local mall or into downtown Boston. Watching and reading people's faces, listening to their conversations, and sometimes engaging them in conversation stretches me to ask if the Christianity I am trying to present to our world is adequate to address the real needs of people.

Listening. Remember one of the four prescriptions that the doctor gave to Arthur Gordon: "Listen carefully"? One of the greatest hindrances in my own growth is my propensity to go for long periods of time without listening. I get so caught up in keeping up with the pace of life that I can go for days without listening to God, to the genuine needs around me, to the birds, or to the inner stirrings of my spirit. When I fail to listen, it usually means that I am failing to think. "Perhaps one of the great needs of this generation," writes Sammy Tippit, "is for thinking men and women. The advent of the computer has brought artificial intelligence to the world. Many Christians have ceased to be thinkers in an age of computers and televisions."[4]

Learning as a lifestyle means making a concerted effort to listen, meditate, and think. We start with our relationship to God. A book like A.W. Tozer's *Knowledge of the Holy* (Harper Religious Books, 1978) helps slow us down long enough to lift our spirits in worship. Some find strength in reading the Scriptures aloud, striving to hear the words afresh. Whether we are helped by hymns, walks in the woods, or getting lost in a crowd, listening to God is a prerequisite for continual growth.

Listening also includes a look within ourselves. Asking ourselves questions like, What is motivating me today? or How am I feeling about life? can put us in touch with some powerful (and frightening) realities about ourselves. Paul Tournier's book, *The Strong and the Weak*,[5] has been one of the best resources I have found in helping me listen inwardly and understand myself.

Learning from listening is incomplete if we are not listening to others. An old sage once stated, "When I's talkin', I ain't learnin' nothin' new." Asking questions, learning from the experience of others, and empathetic listening to hurting people provides on-the-job training in ministry. Even listening to our enemies or our critics is a source of growth. A man I consider a mentor told me, "Even the harshest criticism may contain a granule of truth from which you can learn."

Writing. A peer in youth ministry explained to me why his correspondence was so poor: "I am so full of energy, I never get to sit down and write to you. I am always on the go." I knew his life, and I knew he was telling the truth. He lived on four or five hours sleep a night, and he was the epitome of boundless energy. I envied his metabolism, but after his comment about correspondence, I started to wonder if such boundless energy is a blessing or a curse. Whether he wrote to me was not the point; I wondered if he was slowing down enough to stay in touch with God.

Correspondence illustrates one of the disciplines of learning that fosters spiritual growth. I am not talking about staying in touch with others by mail; I am referring to staying in touch with God through the use of a journal. The great saints of the past are known to us because of their journals, their chronicled insights on their growth with God. We are wise to imitate their example.

Writing in my journal forces me to slow down. If I am too preoccupied to pray, I write my prayers in my journal. When anxiety overpowers me, writing in my journal forces me to ask questions, evaluate the causes, or write out biblical promises longhand.

By writing our prayers and thoughts on paper, we are forced to keep our minds focused on one idea at a time. In addition, this type of thinking on paper can be God's tool for directing our dreams and plans. As we write, we can work through our ideas before God and think through the steps required to achieve certain goals. Writing in a journal helps us experience the promise that "in his heart a man plans his course, but the Lord determines his steps" (Prov. 16:9).

The psalmist wrote, "I will remember the deeds of the Lord" (Psa. 77:11). Writing helps me remember how God has guided or provided in the past, and I am strengthened to face the future with a hitherto-hath-the-Lord-helped-us stimulus.

Writing also helps me to see progress. When I become discouraged, a glance back over an earlier journal entry helps me see victory and growth in areas I had forgotten about. I saw this recently on a birthday review. On my birthday I read back several years to see my entries on previous birthdays. I looked back five years, and I read words that were laced with anger and hostility over issues that I was having difficulty forgiving. My birthday review helped me see progress over the ensuing years to the point where these issues were not even mentioned in last year's entry. My journal showed me that while I am far from being what I should be, at least I am not what I used to be. Growth has occurred.

Getting Away. Busy schedules act like brush fires. They tend to consume whatever is in their path, and without efforts to control them, they increase both in intensity and ability to destroy. Fire fighters battle the blaze, not by combating the fire directly, but by cutting a firebreak, a path in the brush, so that the fire has nothing left to consume. Only by cutting the gap can the fire be brought under control.

When our schedules are burning out of control, we need to create a gap in the landscape, a break in the schedule. Getting away from the office, going to the library, or taking a vacation might be the break we need to slow ourselves down before we are consumed. We all need to get away from our routines for regular time to read, think, plan, and rest. Earl Palmer says his goal is to "divide each week into a rhythm of work, rest, worship, and play: of work with people and work alone; of worship with the community of faith and worship alone; of discussion and reflection. I can take in stride high-intensity demands if there is also built into my life the opportunity for an easing up of demand."[6]

I can tell I need a break when I am living life without rhythms. I see myself as if I were being chased by a nipping dog. The analogy conjures up images of running ahead just enough to keep from being bitten by my pursuers. When hurting people in my ministry, details of planning, or demands of leadership seem to be constantly at my heels, I know it's time to get away from the phones, the mail, the people, even if it's only for one or two hours. I need the time to get my head and heart straight so that I can return to the ministry with greater perspective.

Developing our discipline of learning means striving to get away on a regular basis to add to our ability to prioritize; not every nipping dog needs to be responded to. Time away helps us quiet our spirits. In response to someone else's unreasonable demands or in the face of my own failure, the gentle answer that turns away wrath (Prov. 15:1) emanates from a quiet spirit, not a frenetic one.

When I am stuck in the middle of traffic in the city, I turn on the radio to listen to the reports from the Skyway Patrol. The men or women in the helicopters have the big picture, and their vantage point offers instruction on how to manage my way through the traffic. Time away from the normal routine acts like the Skyway Patrol, giving us a new vantage point so that we can gain perspective on our lives and ministries.

TAKING ACTION

The discipline of learning offers some great ideas, but what will we do about it? Since most youth leaders do not get job descriptions that encourage the implementation of the ideas listed above, consider a few practical steps that may help us in the learning direction.

Reading. Rather than an impossible goal, we can look at our schedules and be realistic. Of all of the books on the to-be-read shelf, choose one. Then set a goal: I want to read this book by (date). Determine how many pages you need to read daily to complete the book, and write on the calendar or in the schedule, Read X pages of (book) every day between now and (the goal date). Some of us may be able to tackle several books at a time, but for me, trying to read regularly from the Bible *plus* one other book is the best I can do on a consistent basis.

When implementing these goals, it is far better to start small, succeed, and then set a higher goal than it is to overwhelm ourselves and quit. Reading five books a week might be our long-term goal, but if in the face of two small children, marriage responsibilities, and the junior-high ministry, five pages a week might be a challenge, we need to start there and build.

In a seminar with youth leaders, I challenged them to read, and since many were interested in improving their management abilities, I suggested they read one book on time management. The group groaned; the challenge seemed overwhelming, so I introduced them to the Youth Specialties book *110 Tips, Timesavers, and Tools of the Trade*, a book of less than one hundred pages with cartoons and large print. It is far better to start small, succeed, and build on the achieved goal than to quit before trying.

Listening and Getting Away. Time away from ministry or time away simply to think and pray is seldom dropped in our laps. We need to plan for it. As a result, the implementation of these two goals means getting out our calendars, looking ahead, and blocking off half a day to study, read, or simply rest. When a new ministry pressure attempts to rob us of that time, respond by saying, "I'm sorry. I have a commitment that day." To put this into practice, support from our spouse or secretary is crucial. A secretary who protects this time by covering for us is far superior to one who responds to a caller, "I don't know where he is. I think he's off on one of his stupid walks in the woods again!"

Since the realities of ministry make time away to listen and be refreshed hard-to-reach goals, I recommend trying to block out three to five hours on every week's schedule. The inevitable interruptions of people-work may cause us to lose a few of these hours, but even two three-hour blocks in a five-week period might be better than we are doing now. It may take us a decade to establish the rhythms recommended by Earl Palmer, but let's at least try to improve our current situation

Writing. How do we start (or resume) the discipline of writing in a prayer journal? When I fall out of the habit, I go out and buy a new notebook and try to write a summary of my growth during the days I missed. I commence with a little inventory of what is going on in my spiritual growth at that point so that in days ahead I can build on it. Rewriting a prayer list, copying a favorite Scripture text, or writing a collection of favorite quotations from books on the spiritual life might be the place to start.

Again I recommend simplicity. Try writing one paragraph each day. Write a prayer for the day, or that evening, thanking God for the day. Since writing like this is a discipline, don't worry if it doesn't get easier. Give it a try and see if it helps in guiding thoughts and directing growth. After a month or two, if it is nothing but tediousness, drop it and look for a way to track growth that works better for you.

BEATING THE HAS-BEEN TRAP

When we are called to look into our spirits and examine the fruitfulness of our minds, will we find that we look like a has-been in the old-timers game? Will we be forced to reminisce about the days when we used to learn? Or will we look fresh, committed to growth, delighted to be maturing? Committing ourselves to take an aggressive stance toward growth will make the difference.

CHAPTER TEN
BALANCE: SETTING PRIORITIES IN THE FACE OF DECISION OVERLOAD

Most of us live in a constant state of choosing. While a poor person in a Third World ghetto suffers because he has no options, we struggle because we have too many. Our abundance of options leads to lives that are expended on multiple choices rather than focusing on one or two priorities. Many of us are spiritually and psychologically fatigued. Ruth Graham, Billy Graham's wife, calls the modern evangelical "packed man." We have so many options that we are paralyzed by too many choices and fatigued by trying to carry out too much, too soon, too fast, too often.

Gail MacDonald illustrates the same point with a story in *Keep Climbing* about a woman who returned after four years in a developing country. When asked about her greatest reentry shock, the woman commented on the overwhelming number of choices in the supermarket, where an entire aisle was dedicated to varieties of potato chips. "My friends aren't even aware of the energy it's taking, they've gotten so used to the subtle enslavement. So you asked what has shocked me? It's seeing the time wasted over 'potato chip decisions,' so that when the truly important issues need our attention, our energies have already been squandered on trivia."[1]

The bottom line is *balance*. With so many choices bombarding us from every angle of life, how can we stay balanced in our growth? Where do we invest our energies? How do we spend our time? Do we respond to every emergency, or do we let people take care of themselves?

Spiritual health, like physical health, requires a balanced diet, exercise, and time. We need a consistent diet of spiritual input, exercise in spiritual disciplines, and appropriate time to think and pray. But how does this work out in our lives?

A DOSE
OF REALITY

What does it mean to be a balanced, healthy, growing youth leader? If we imagine a youth worker who looks as vibrant as the people who make vitamin commercials, we will be deeply disappointed. I have met many men and women whose spiritual health is apparent in their lives, but I have never met anyone who I would call the picture of a balanced life.

Someone may respond, "But look at Jesus. The Bible says that Jesus did all things well. Surely he is the picture of balance." Indeed he is, but since I have never met anyone who looks one hundred percent like Jesus, I reiterate that there is no one who is perfectly balanced. The life Jesus exemplified is a target we aim for, not a goal we achieve on this earth.

A single youth-worker friend and I were going out to lunch, and I suggested that we take his car. He blanched at the thought, but I could not understand why. Then I got to his car. As I opened the passenger-side door, stacks of coffee cups, empty bags from McDonald's, donut wrappers, and other trash tumbled out. It was obvious that he was accustomed to driving alone. My seeing the trash was embarrassment enough for my friend. As I cleared a path to sit down, I said, "Don't worry, Fred. All of us have messy corners in our lives; I just happened to stumble onto yours."

All of us have our messy corners. No one achieves the totally balanced lives we aspire for. We can grow in the right direction, but even growth often reveals new "messy corners" of our spirits that never used to bother us. This is the process known as sanctification.

Understanding ourselves realistically in the pursuit of balance demands that we take two important factors into account. First, we need to consider the seasons of our lives. Balance looks different for a single youth worker than it does for a married couple with three children under the age of five. A rookie youth worker will have different goals than a twenty-year veteran.

While looking for better ways of time management one year, I read the manual *Time Management for Youth Workers*. I was looking for new ways to improve my use of time, and there were some helpful tips. But when the author suggested sleeping in the car as a way to save time, I realized I was reading the words of a single man who was in a different season of life than I was.

The second important factor is to recognize that *God's* standard of balance for us might be different than the standard set for us by *others*. As a result, we need courage to keep from feeling poorly about ourselves because we do not measure up to ideals set for us by others. Ultimately, our sense of balance must come from a sense of God's direction in our personal growth.

EXAMPLES OF BALANCE

The youth worker with the trash-filled front seat refused my consolation and asked, "But where are your messy corners?" He thought that my life was together, but he had never seen me snap at Christie over some insignificant trifle when I was in a bad mood.

Consider three areas that need juggling as we try to balance our lives in the face of competing time demands.

Personal time versus ministry time. One of the critical areas where we cannot tolerate messy corners is our primary relationships, marriage, or family. If our relationships at home suffer because of neglect, our entire ministry suffers.

One seven-days-a-week-with-the-kids youth minister told me that I was in danger of deifying the family. He assured me that he knew God was going to take care of his wife and children while he served other peoples' kids. The man virtually ignored his family under the guise of serving Christ. The imbalance of his life finally caught up with him. His wife, in spite of her commitment to Christ and her commitment to her husband, responded to the love of another man and left town. The youth minister is now bitter, thinking that God did not hold up his end of the bargain.

On the opposite end of the spectrum, an associate minister so treasured his family that he told the church, "I will not be out more than two nights per week." As he enjoyed his family more and more, the minister took more and more time to work at home. His ministry suffered from neglect; his teaching was satisfactory, but he fell out of touch with his people. Eventually the church told him to enjoy his family as much as he wanted, but not at their expense. They fired him.

Both examples illustrate the dangers of neglecting imbalances in our personal versus ministry time. Most of us are prone to err like the first man, but both men illustrate the ends of the spectrum that represent imbalance.

Karen Hutchcraft, veteran of youth ministry with her husband Ron, writes,

> One of the major lessons I learned early in our youth-work partnership is that an effective ministry is a by-product of a secure marriage. Youth workers are often underappreciated and overcriticized. They are besieged with impossible expectations. All that can be pretty rough on the ego. When a youth leader walks into his home, he doesn't need another battleground where he has to defend or promote something. What he needs at home is a safe sanctuary.[2]

The home that Karen Hutchcraft describes, however, is a result of a balanced investment by her husband, Ron. When, in the words of another youth leader, our homes degenerate into "a fast-food restaurant and a place to sleep,"[3] the imbalance will destroy the comradery and partnership of the marriage and home.

Veteran youth worker Ridge Burns suggests seven ways to balance ministry and family life.

1. Take time to talk with your spouse and family about your ministry.
2. Put your family on the mailing list so that they can help you deal with conflicts.
3. Schedule a family weekend away each year.
4. Schedule a three-month sabbatical every four years of ministry. (Ideal, but worth suggesting!)
5. Set aside a night per week with your family to ask, "How are we getting along?"
6. Do something outside the ministry with your spouse or family that is fun.
7. Travel together. Whenever possible, bring your family with you to conferences or seminars.[4]

Thought time versus activity time. Balancing the need to study with the need to be with students creates tension. We may favor one over the other, even if we know that both are needed. Dan favors time with students. He loves students so much that his reading and study time suffers when he is not careful. After approaching several ministry opportunities Dan, realizing that he was unprepared to teach, decided that he needed to discipline himself and add some study and thinking time into his schedule. For him, a balance in this area is spending three hours a week reading and studying.

Mark is exactly the opposite. He loves to study, dream, and think. If left to himself, Mark could go for two or three weeks away from people. As a youth leader, however, he knows he needs to be with students as well as with the adults who serve

FEEDING YOUR FORGOTTEN SOUL

with him. For him, balance is two nights a week at student activities and one night with the youth-leadership team.

Time with adults versus time with students. Time with people is one of the primary tools for influencing their lives, but it is also one of the primary ways by which we respond. As a result, we need to make sure to balance our time with students (whom we can challenge to grow) with our time with adults (who can challenge us to grow with them as peers).

Mary spends most of her time with her youth-leadership team. After ten years with the youth group, she feels she can maximize her impact on students by influencing the adults who lead them. Scott spends most of his time with students. He believes in a direct-impact style of leadership, so he delegates the leadership of adult coworkers to an associate.

Mary runs the risk of spending too much time with adults and not enough with students. While Mary might have great rapport with her coworkers (and possibly with the parents of her students), the negative results of this imbalance might include

- Loss of empathy with students' needs and problems.
- Students who feel she has left them.
- Loss of credibility with teenagers and familiarity with the teen world.
- Increased impatience with adolescent behavior.
- Inability to teach effectively using illustrations teenagers understand.

Scott, on the other hand, tends to develop great rapport with students. His teaching reflects his knowledge of their world and his empathy with their problems; but his imbalance might also have negative results that include

- An increased tendency to behave like an adolescent himself.

- An inability to relate to and learn from peers.
- A loss of credibility with adult volunteers and with parents of youths.
- An increased tendency to defend teenagers, even when their behavior is indefensible.

Healthy growth means balancing time spent with those that we can influence positively with time spent with those who positively influence us.

STAYING ON CENTER

Our abundance of choices makes balance an elusive pursuit. Messy corners abound, but the discipline of spiritual growth is, in the words of Anne Morrow Lindbergh, "how to remain *whole* in the midst of the distractions of life; how to remain *balanced*, no matter what centrifugal forces tend to pull one off center; how to remain *strong*, no matter what shocks come in at the periphery and tend to crack the hub of the wheel."[5]

Striving for wholeness, balance, and strength characterizes the person dedicated to spiritual health. Now let's look at some practical tools to assist us in our efforts.

SECTION
THREE

SPIRITUAL GROWTH FOR THE LONG HAUL

Earlier I shared my horror when I came face-to-belly with my vacation photographs. I had to do something about the dough boy I was becoming, so I sought some advice at a local gym. A man my age consulted with me and summed up his advice by saying, "You will find that getting in shape may not be your biggest problem; the problem will be *staying* in shape."

The same is true in our spiritual growth. Getting in shape may not be the problem. We can recognize our need and respond with disciplines, exercises, and proactive resolves that may last a few days, weeks, or even months. The problem will be maintaining a level of positive spiritual growth over the long haul. Developing Christ-like responses *once* may not be a challenge, but sustaining a Christ-like spirit certainly is.

We recognize the pitfalls of youth-ministry life. We understand the challenges we face regarding spiritual disciplines. Now what will we do? How do we start to make progress in the right direction? The next chapters offer some practical suggestions—ideas that will assist our spiritual growth and ongoing health if we remember a few basic foundations.

Growth is not so much an achieved goal as it is a direction. Getting in shape spiritually may never occur totally; there will always be areas in which we recognize that we could grow more, read more, pray more, or serve more. Even if the growth seems minuscule, we can take courage. We are moving in the right direction.

Uniform progress may not occur. The seasons of our spiritual growth will vary widely. We will stumble and fall, but growth is the commitment to get back up. When we go for weeks without a commitment to spiritual growth, our return to health will be determined by whether we lament our state and think, There's no hope for me, or we come back to Jesus, ask him to dust us off, and look to him for the renewed motivation we need.

The grass is not *always greener in the other person's yard.* Some will read this book, focus on the hurdles of youth work, and decide, That settles it; I have got to resign youth ministry. Youth ministry is harming me spiritually.

Resigning is not the only option. We can turn things around. If quitting is the only option, where is our gospel of hope? Some of the resolves we can make within our own specific context can turn us in the right direction.

One of the toughest lessons we'll ever learn is that life in general and ministry in particular are difficult. I have watched some leave youth ministry too early, blaming youth ministry for realities that are actually a result of normal adult life.

One of the characteristics of biblical heroes was perseverance. In the book of Daniel, our hero endured foreign domination under four kings. Moses persevered and saw the Promised Land, if only from a distance. Elizabeth, Hannah, and Sarah had to wait before they saw the child they so desperately wanted. Jesus, because of the vision he had before him, endured the ultimate rejection of the Cross.

WINNING THE RACE

Robert Service, the poet laureate of the Yukon, wrote a poem titled "The Men That Don't Fit In." I loved the title, so I looked through the local library until I found it. Rather than telling me what I had expected—that it was the "men that don't fit in" who changed the world—he stated quite the opposite. The "men that don't fit in" wander the world aimlessly, restlessly trying to sink their roots, but without success. Service concluded that it was the "steady, quiet, plodding ones who win the lifelong race."

To be a steady, quiet plodding one sounds neither romantic nor adventurous, but they are the characteristics that result in effective spiritual growth and effective ministry to youths. To endure rather than to live for the quick fix presents a long-term challenge.

In the words of Longfellow,

> The heights by great men reached and kept
> Were not obtained by sudden flight;
> But they, while their companions slept
> Were toiling upwards in the night.

Perseverance. Getting in shape may not be our problem; it is staying in shape. Go for it!

CHAPTER ELEVEN
PERSEVERANCE: ARMING FOR THE SEXUAL BATTLE

On a flight from Atlanta to Boston, I noticed that the man in the seat ahead of me was reading *Playboy*. As (I confess!) I peeked through the space between the seats, I caught glimpses of some memorable pictures. After several minutes the man put the magazine away (assisting in my sanctification), and to my amazement, immediately took out his Bible and began to have his quiet time. He read the Scriptures and bowed his head in prayer, all within minutes of perusing the sensual pictures in *Playboy*.

The inconsistency amazed me. But I realized all of the fingers I pointed at him were pointing back at me. The spiritual split personality that he so boldly demonstrated was equally true in my own life. The only difference was that I was more discreet.

The battle against lust, inconsistency, and sexual temptation will know no end, at least not in this life. To engage in the battle that wages war against our souls is a lifetime challenge that demands full armaments for battle.

> AXIOM: Perseverance in the battle against lust and sexual sin demands honesty, humility, and a long-term commitment.

SUITING UP

Until now I have been referring to the obstacles to spiritual growth as hurdles. Since sexual temptation is so intense, I have moved in this chapter to military analogies such as battles, attack, and waging war.

To be honest, I do not know of any guaranteed solution to lust or sexual sin. The best perspective I have learned is to think of it as a lifetime battle. Rather than thinking of myself as having won, I prefer to work toward being able to say, "Today I am winning." The following suggestions can help us stay on the winning side of the battle.

Seek forgiveness and restoration. Gordon MacDonald, writing from firsthand experience in *Rebuilding Your Broken World*, encourages us all to see ourselves as "broken world people." Until we are willing to say, "Yes, Lord, it is I in need of your special grace and mercy in this matter," we will be unable to build our defenses for the future.

When Lee, an eighty-four-year-old visiting speaker, came to Grace Chapel one summer, people were casually dressed in shorts and tank tops. Members of our leadership team prayed with him before the seminar. I will never forget his honest and vulnerable prayer: "Lord, with these women in their shorts and tank tops, I pray that you will deliver me from lustful thinking." I was amazed. This aging man of God who had been a Christian over sixty years admitted that he was still struggling with lust.

In a private discussion afterwards, I asked him about victory over lust. He encouraged me to memorize Proverbs 28:13: "He who conceals his sins does not prosper, but whoever *confesses and renounces* them finds mercy." He exhorted me to keep coming back to Jesus for forgiveness again and again.

Seeking God is not the immediate cure. The anonymous author of one of *Leadership* magazine's most popular articles, "The War Within: An Anatomy of Lust," told his story of defeat against lust. "You know what it is like to wallow in the guilt of that obsession, to plead with God to release you, to mutate you, to castrate you like Origen—whatever it takes to deliver you.

And even as you pray, luscious, bewitching images crowd into your mind."[1]

But six year later, the same writer offered hope in his sequel, "The War Within Continues."

I cannot tell you why a prayer that has been prayed for ten years is answered on the 1,000th request when God has met the first 999 with silence. I cannot tell you why I had to endure ten years of near-possession before being ready for deliverance . . . But what I can tell you, especially those of you who have hung on every turn of my pilgrimage because it so closely corresponds to yours, is that God did come through for me. The phrase may sound heretical, but to me, after so many years of failure, it felt as if He had suddenly decided to be there after a long absence. I prayed, hiding nothing from God (hide from God?), and He heard me.[2]

If you're married, talk honestly with your spouse. Nothing has been more remedial to me than honest confession, discussion, and prayer with my wife about this matter. When I travel she prays that I will not be in a hotel room that has pay television. If there is, I tell her, and she encourages me to keep the TV off. She asks, "Is this too much for you?" when we are watching a movie or TV show that is sexually provocative. And she responds to my answer without calling me a pervert or a sex maniac.

My best retardant to lustful thinking, sneaking a glimpse at pornography, or masturbation has been honest conversation with my wife. I am capable of leading myself into moral destruction if my only concern is myself, but my love for my wife curtails my temptations because it forces me to think, I don't want to do this to *her*.

Don't rationalize. Several years ago I became aware of two very close friends who resigned their ministry positions because of adultery. The most shocking part of the discovery was how well they had kept things hidden, first from their spouses, then from friends, then from people in their ministries. In the midst of the hidden time, both were maintaining effective ministries. The experience reminded me of our awful abilities to compartmentalize our lives. To borrow an analogy from Robert Munger's *My Heart, Christ's Home*, it is as though we are able to entertain Jesus happily in the living room while everything going on in the bedroom is in direct opposition to his purposes.

A number of years ago, before the popularization of videos and cable TV, I tried to stay relevant with students by going to the theater to see the movies that they were watching. When Bo Derek's *10* (a movie built on her sexual attractiveness) was released, I found myself asking students if they had been to see it. In my self-deceit, I was hoping to accumulate enough affirmative answers to justify my going to see it. In effect, I wanted to escape responsibility for my lusts by blaming the students.

The temptation to rationalize has intensified now that we no longer need to go to the movie theater. Instead of driving to see an immoral movie, we invite the movie into our homes through VCRs and cable stations.

We all have a staggering capacity to rationalize, cover our errant behavior, and act (the essence of the word hypocrisy) as if nothing is wrong. Rather than identifying our weak spots, we excuse them and open ourselves to the most frightening deceit of all—self-deceit.

Run. Jack, a veteran youth worker, told me how he was once watching a rented movie with his three teenage sons. When the sexy scenes came on, Jack told his sons, "I don't know about you guys, but I can't watch this without lusting," and he left the room. He let his sons make up their own minds, and they soon followed their Dad's honesty; they shut the movie off.

We all need to take our example from Joseph who, after days of being tempted and seduced by Potiphar's wife, escaped the only way he could—he ran. Paul exhorted Timothy to "flee youthful lusts" (2 Tim. 2:22). If Joseph and Timothy dealt with lust by running, why don't we?

Spiritual maturity means running. At the newsstand, buy the newspaper and run. Do not linger, drifting towards the adult magazines as if it were an accident. Alone in a hotel room? Run from the cable movies or pay TV; rely on the radio for the news and weather. Sexual temptation should not be flirted with. Thumbing through *Playboy* under the guise of reading the articles is asking for trouble. Even if we escape unscathed on that encounter, we enter pictures into our photographic memory banks that our minds can recall later. It is far better to run.

Be accountable. Mike came to our youth ministry as an adult volunteer. He was instantly popular with our students, and many of our neediest students gravitated towards him. Jill, an attractive young woman, was especially drawn towards Mike. He became the father figure that she had always wanted, and I noticed that Mike was becoming increasingly attracted to her. Her innocence made him quite vulnerable, but I had no real grounds for confronting him. Mike and I started to meet together regularly. When we started committing ourselves to growing together, I shared my concern.

At the first confrontation, Mike denied anything other than a personal concern for Jill. After all, he reasoned, he was twelve years older than she and happily married with a child on the way. "She's just a child," he laughed. But two weeks later, Mike thanked me for the confrontation. He had prayed about it and was forced to come to grips with the fact that as irrational as it seemed, he was infatuated with Jill. He knew it was wrong, but his emotions were telling him otherwise.

We talked through the issue and eventually, because I was holding him accountable for his actions, Mike slowly began to distance himself from Jill. I had pointed out the unhealthy aspects of the relationship, but he had to make the decision to get out of it.

If we plan to stay clear from personal sin, we need help, and the help should be from more than just our spouses. Men need men and women need women who can ask each other hard questions. Sometimes just the knowledge that a friend holds me accountable for my actions is enough to keep me on the narrow path of following Christ.

Keep perspective. God loves us more than our ministries. I once met a youth leader who was being consumed over the grief and despair of a past sexual sin and a renewed sexual temptation. The incident had occurred five years earlier at his current ministry, but the person with whom he had sinned had just returned to the area, rekindling all sorts of reactions. "What are you doing to get help?" I asked him.

"No one near me even knows," he said. "If someone found out, my ministry would be over, and the kids would be devastated."

His reply is sadly accurate, at least in practical, human terms. But he is overlooking one basic spiritual truth: God loves us, not our ministries, not our performance, and not our successes. As soon as we equate our ministries with our walk with Christ, we are inviting spiritual disaster. God's first priority is to make us whole through Jesus. He sent Jesus to die for our sins; we do not need to die for them also.

I am not trying to sound naive or simplistic. I simply want to emphasize that God's love reaches us no matter what the sin.

Staying Pure. Paul exhorted Timothy to be an example to the believers at the church in Ephesus by purity (1 Tim. 4:12). In his culture there were those who mixed prostitution with worship and sexual promiscuity with business. Timothy's culture was as sexually saturated as ours, yet Paul still exhorted him to purity.

When we grow tired of waging spiritual warfare and think, No one in biblical times encountered what I encounter, we should remember Timothy. He serves as a reminder that God will make us capable of obeying his commands whatever the outside pressures. If we arm ourselves for battle, God will give us long-term victory.

CHAPTER TWELVE
APPRAISAL: A SANE VIEW OF MYSELF

One of the great ongoing challenges of life is to follow Socrates' advice, "Know thyself." Who am I? Where am I going? Why am I doing youth work? What is God's call on my life? If we are seriously trying to understand God and his call, these and other questions will loom large.

Building for long-term spiritual growth and health means recognizing where we are both in our personal lives and in our service to God.

> AXIOM: With a realistic appraisal of where we are
> strong and where we need help, we can begin to build
> for our personal progress.

When the folks at Grace Chapel first invited me to undertake the leadership of the youth ministry, I turned them down. My predecessor was dynamic, a good singer, an excellent speaker, and quite charismatic in his ability to lead. I perceived none of these qualities or skills in myself, and I knew that I would be crushed by the comparison.

A year later they came to me again. Over the months that had passed, the youth group had gone through four different leaders and a very difficult transition. During the same time, I had come to understand myself. I knew that I could not compare myself to my predecessor, but I also knew that God had equipped me, perhaps in different ways that he now wanted to use. I accepted the position.

One of the key contributors to my growth at that time was Paul Tournier's book, *The Strong and the Weak*. An honest appraisal of myself emerged out of his assertion that "all men, in fact, are weak. All are weak because all are afraid. They are afraid of being trampled underfoot. They are all afraid of their inner weakness being discovered. They all have secret faults; they all have a bad conscience on account of certain acts which they would like to keep covered up. They are all afraid of other men and of God, of life and of death."[1]

When we realize that we are sinners, that we fail as much as we succeed, that we are broken because of our past mistakes or present fears, then we are ready to grow. Jesus summarized it in Matthew 5:3: "How happy are those who *know their need of God*; the kingdom of Heaven belongs to them" (New English Bible).

WE NEED HELP

Acknowledging brokenness is never easy, especially in a society where only the outwardly successful are honored. In our ministry leadership and even before God, we are all prone to present an image that is far greater than the actual state of our souls. To build a realistic appraisal of who we are spiritually, we need help. Consider four essential themes or disciplines that must run through our lives to maintain a level-headed view of where we are strong, where we need to grow, and where we need help.

Humility. Several years ago, our youth ministry hosted an evangelism seminar for youth leaders. We housed the visiting leaders in the homes of active students so that these visitors could talk with students directly. One leader stayed with a sophomore named Jon. When the leader mentioned articles I had written and seminars I had led, Jon responded, "Paul Borthwick? He's just the bald guy who runs the youth group!" God had sent Jon to keep me humble.

Humility is basically a fair estimate of our strengths and weaknesses. It is not a groveling self-denigration that reduces us to nothing, but it is a full recognition that all that we have or are comes from God. We are free to realize the spiritual progress we have made, but humility is the recognition that no one seeks for God except by God's initiative (Rom. 3:11). We are free to recognize our spiritual gifts and abilities, but humility means acknowledging that they are God's gifts (see 1 Cor. 4:7).

Humility is realizing that God has made us leaders of others while nervously acknowledging that their spirituality is, at least in part, a reflection of the example that we have set before them. Leroy Eims, a leader for the Navigators, addresses this theme with respect to Moses' call to leadership in Exodus 3 and 4. "Moses, it really doesn't matter who you are—whether you feel qualified or unqualified, whether you feel up to the task or not. The point is that *I* am going to be there . . . I am going to deliver them, and I am going to give you the privilege of being in it with me."[2]

As we build our own spiritual growth (and presumably for the spiritual health of those we serve), humility releases us to admit our shortcomings, although we realize that God is sufficient. He does not require dynamism or charisma; instead, he requires our availability to him. Being just "the bald guy who runs the youth group" is enough.

Harvey, a partner in ministry, explained humility to me using the example of Nehemiah. One the characteristics of Nehemiah is that the hand of God was upon him. Harvey put his hand on my shoulder and asked, "Paul, how much effort does it take for me to remove my hand from you?"

I concluded that it took little or no effort. Harvey observed, "That shows how easy it would be for God to remove his hand from us. When we realize all that we have and are is a result of God's hand on us, and we recognize how easily he can remove his hand, we are in a humble posture where we can grow."

Integration. Put simply, are we living what we are teaching? With the information explosion and all of the resources available to us through books, videos, tapes, and conferences, it is easy for us to teach and talk far beyond our experience.

At the Lausanne II Conference in Manila, Luis Palau, the evangelist from Latin America, closed the conference with these words: "We have spent the last ten days talking about evangelism, but how many of us have been doing it?" He made his point to the four-thousand-plus attenders: Talking about evangelism is easier than doing it.

Leadership has an illusionary quality to it. I can imagine that if I have taught it, I have lived it. If I can write about it, I must have mastered it. If students say I am their spiritual leader, it must be true. Correct? Not necessarily. As leaders we can (to paraphrase C.S. Lewis) imagine spiritual conditions far beyond anything we have actually lived. In the process of explaining to others what we have imagined, we can convince them and ourselves that we have actually been there.

Without asking the question, "Am I living what I teach?" we can fall prey to the illusion that our spiritual growth is much further along than it actually is. As leaders we need to be sobered by the realization that we "will be judged more strictly" (James 3:1). In other words, we cannot be content with living eighty percent of what we teach. The stricter-judgment principle implies that we should be better than what we teach others to be, living one hundred ten percent of our teaching. An appraisal of our consistency in integrating what we teach is bound to assist us in developing humility!

Attitudes. Spiritual growth requires that we go against the stream of feelings and discipline ourselves to do what is right, even when we do *not* feel like it. This growth is what builds our character in Christ. Listen to the challenge of Eims again: "The inner life of the leader will either make him or break him. If he neglects the cultivation of purity, humility, and faith, he is in for big trouble."[3] The inner life, our attitudes, is reflected in how we treat loved ones, how we respond to the needy person, how we approach God each time we pause to pray.

There are two basic attitudinal positions that I have observed in myself. The first harms my spiritual health; the second builds it. When I spend time thinking of all the "thank-yous" parents or students owe me, I manifest an attitude of entitlement. This attitude makes me think that growth, good things, and fulfillment are things that are due me. When one of my perceived rights is crossed, either by another person or by God—when he does not seem to hold up what I perceive to be his part of the bargain—I grow bitter, caustic, or disillusioned.

The disciples may have approached an attitude of entitlement towards Jesus. They reasoned that God's Messiah would overthrow the Roman oppressor. Even when Jesus was about to ascend, they were still asking, "Are you going to establish the kingdom now?" (Acts 1:6). Their disillusionment, illustrated on the Emmaus road—"*We had hoped* that he was the one who was going to redeem Israel" (Luke 24:21)—may have lasted ten days before the real work of the Holy Spirit began.

When we who lead youths feel trapped by our choice to serve youths, feel insulted by parents who refuse to acknowledge our adulthood, or feel bored by the repetition, it could be because we have adopted an unhealthy attitude of entitlement that leads us to say . . .

- I had hoped that life would get easier or at least that it would be more exciting.
- I had hoped that there would be greater respect for me and my calling.
- I had hoped that there would be faster results in the lives of students and families.

The alternative to entitlement is an attitude of servitude. I once infuriated a visiting youth worker because I did not memorize his two-paragraph list of credentials that he wanted me to recite to the audience before he came to speak. The experience made me appreciate a youth worker who comes as a worker for Jesus, a servant of Jesus. I respect the spirit of a servant. Blessed are the unassuming! Mary, the mother of Jesus, illustrates this attitude best when she responds to the angelic announcement, "I am the Lord's servant. May it be to me as you have said" (Luke 1:38). She made no demands, insisted on no rights. She knew her Lord and submitted.

If we reach the point in our ministries where we are saying such things as "I would never take a smaller ministry," "I have outgrown these people," or "I am not as appreciated as I should be," we should beware lest we construct prideful obstacles in our spiritual pathway. When we cease to consider ourselves servants, we create a force field that prohibits our spiritual progress.

Self-criticism. Our former pastor frequently encouraged those of us on staff to practice ruthless self-criticism. By this he meant taking a hard look at ourselves without excusing our weaknesses or pampering our shortcomings. He wanted us to grow, and he knew that many decisions for growth are ultimately decisions of the will. If we are not tough on ourselves, we gladly tolerate standards far below our actual potential.

We need to review the previous chapters and say, "I have been too easy on myself by blaming the spiritual hurdles of youth ministry for my spiritual malaise; I need to discipline myself to act on what I know!" It may mean confession: "Lord, forgive me for pampering myself instead of challenging myself as a soldier of Jesus Christ."

The apostle Paul referred to disciplining himself harshly lest after preaching to others, he should be disqualified (1 Cor. 9:24-27). He knew the grace of God, but he also knew the demands of following Jesus and did not want to find himself out of shape on the final stretch of the race. Building spiritual growth over the long haul requires honest confrontations within ourselves. Do we really want to grow? If so, are we willing to come face to face with our shortcomings and ask God to help us win over them? If not, are we willing to wait until he gives us the desire to grow?

When the *Rocky* movies were popular, I remember looking with awe at the physical specimen Sylvester Stallone had made himself into. When I saw *Rocky III*, I realized that Stallone was older than I, and I told my wife, "That's what I would like to look like." Then after the movie I said, "Let's go out for an ice cream sundae." I wanted the results—Stallone's physical condition—but I had no desire to confront what it cost to get there.

Some of the preceding chapters may have stirred up spiritual desires. We may find ourselves thinking, that's what I would like to be like. Ruthless self-criticism enables us to say: "Here is where I am; there is where I would like to be; and this is what it will take to move from here to there."

LAYING THE FOUNDATION

Who am I? Do I understand who God has made me to be—with all my respective strengths and weaknesses? Am I humble enough to admit in which direction I need to grow and honest enough to accept the challenge? Am I courageous enough to admit the areas of my life in which I need to integrate the teaching I pass on to others? Am I willing to be a servant? As we march forward in the lifelong goal of spiritual health, an open assessment of where we are will provide the foundation on which we can build.

CHAPTER THIRTEEN
PACING: A MARATHONER'S PERSPECTIVE

Youth ministry has many sprinters—young, strong men and women who can achieve amazing speed over a short period of time. But where are they after two or three or five years? We need more marathon runners. Youth leaders may be slow at the starting line, but like the tortoise in the fable, their long-term perseverance helps them endure and win the race. John Sanford addresses this issue in *Ministry Burnout*.

> A ministering person enters his profession, not for just a few years, but with the expectation of serving for a lifetime. For this reason he must find a way to work at a pace that can be maintained for a long period of time. He must learn to think like a long-distance runner, who knows he has a long way to run and cannot afford to exhaust himself by running the first part of the race faster than a pace he can maintain.[1]

The key to a marathon perspective toward our spiritual growth is a long-term outlook on our lives. We do not have to achieve every objective by age thirty or thirty-five. There is a lot of life to be lived, and pacing ourselves enables us to endure. In this long-term view, we see each day as a short race within the marathon of life. To keep moving forward, we grow by setting measurable goals that enhance our progress.

> AXIOM: Spiritual health over a lifetime is built on personal pace-setting and running each day of the race faithfully.

TARGET
PRACTICE

While spirituality cannot be crassly reduced to a set of goals and objectives, we can set targets for our spiritual pilgrimage and ask God to guide us forward. Even though goal-setting sounds like a business term, it can prove valuable to us as we work for sustained spiritual health. Goal setting acts as a catalyst to our spiritual lives. The achievement of goals does not guarantee spiritual maturity any more than a good map and a set of directions gets us where we want to go. Goals help us lay out the map and the directions. As we travel forward, God can use our work toward these goals to help us to grow spiritually.

Goal setting also helps us see measurable results. The goals that we set and achieve enable us to see progress as well as shortcomings in our spiritual pilgrimage. Goals show us where we have come from and where we need to go.

Finally, goal setting helps us set patterns in our lives. If we set a goal to read through the New Testament this year, we develop not only a greater knowledge of the Scriptures, but also a daily pattern of Bible reading, a pattern that God can use to erode the rough and sinful corners of our lives.

A LIFE GOAL?

Goal-setting specialists like Ted Engstrom and Ed Dayton advocate the establishment of a life goal. This is a difficult concept, especially since few of us can anticipate more than three to five years into the future. Nevertheless, a day away in prayer and reflection, asking God, "What should I set as my life goal?" helps us do some healthy long-term thinking. One friend told me that his life goal was to last. He made the comment after several close associates had dropped out of ministry due to failures in integrity. His life goal, though negatively inspired, illustrated his desire to be a spiritual marathon runner.

When someone pushes me to identify my life goal, I respond with, "To be a motivator of others towards world missions." Even my ministry to youth is motivated by a desire to disciple them to be world Christians, able to integrate their faith to be able to affect our world for Christ. Gail MacDonald tells of a woman whose life goal was simply to choose life. The woman explained that "we can eat a candy bar or an apple, but which will lead to a greater quality of health? We can watch TV or read a book, but which leads to a greater quality of growth? We can say the loving word or the critical word, but which conveys the quality of personal nourishment?"[2]

A life goal identifies a personal sense of overarching purpose. It is not a simple Christian standard that applies to all Christians—to obey Jesus, for example. It is more than that; it is a statement of something we feel uniquely qualified by God to do. A life goal has practical ramifications as well. The man who wants to last must build his personal relationship with Jesus so that he can stay faithful daily. The woman who says, "Choose life," dedicates herself to helping others choose life as well have a relationship with Jesus Christ. If I desire to motivate others toward world missions, I must be sure that I am growing in that direction and that I am developing solid relationships with the people I desire to influence.

LIFE SENTENCE

Long-term thinking and discussing life goals inevitably raises the question, "Am I called to youth ministry for life?" Some ask it with a foreboding sense that youth ministry is a sentence from which they hope to be eventually paroled. Others who worry about the future want an easy answer since they find great security in their youth-ministry leadership role.

I have met men and women who have had a strong conviction that they were called to lifetime youth ministry. But in some cases, I sensed a reactionary attitude toward those that started and retired in youth ministry after eight months. Others like Bill Stewart, Von Trutschler, Dave Koser, and Les Christie illustrate a lifetime call to youth ministry without talking too much about it.

An unmarried youth-worker friend (now seventy years old) helped me resolve the issue. He said, "To say I am called to lifetime youth ministry is like saying I am called to singleness. Throughout the course of my life, I have considered many relationships as potentials towards marriage, but at each juncture, God clearly directed me back to my single state. Now that I'm seventy, I think I can affirm that God has called me to lifetime singleness, but even five years ago, I probably would not have said that.

"In the same way," he went on, "I can now say that I have been called to lifetime youth ministry. I have considered many other offers over the years — pastoral leadership, administrative positions, teaching posts — but each time God clearly directed me back to youth work."

Some readers may disagree, vehemently arguing that they know at age twenty-eight that they are called to lifetime youth ministry. No problem. Call me when you are seventy!

When we set a life goal, it is wisest to focus on character traits or general ministry goals. My life goal, for example, gives me the freedom to be a mission-minded youth worker, a youth-minded mission worker, a pastor, or a lay leader dedicated to affecting the lives of others. If my goal were more specified to be a youth-mission-team specialist, it might be so specific that I would feel uncomfortable if I sensed God were leading me to grow and serve in a different direction.

LIFE-VIEW
GOAL SETTING

Building long-term spiritual health means doing some evaluation. Consider some questions I repeatedly ask myself to stir my thinking about what the long-term view of my life should be.

Why am I in youth ministry? Understanding that God has called us to where we are today helps us build for tomorrow. If we have no answer to this question, we need to spend time on the basic question of God's call. Early in my youth ministry, I realized that I was in youth ministry because of the powerful impact that other youth leaders had on me. I wanted to affect the lives of teenagers in the same way that they had affected me. As I grew, however, I developed a greater sense that God had called me to youth ministry. When I started thinking, I realized God directed me to commit myself to one generation of high schoolers at a time. Rather than multiple years of youth ministry, I had multiple commitments to respective generations of teenagers.

In light of this generational perspective, I would set my growth goals accordingly. Evaluating the call (in my case in four-year increments) helped me to set goals over that same time period. Since I was committed to the next four years, I could set growth goals within that time frame. Looking at one small chunk of the broad span known as the future, I could set goals simply by completing the phrase, In four years, I would like to be . . . , I would like to have done . . . , or I would like to have learned . . .

Asking why may help us in a more basic way. Taking the time to evaluate God's call may allow us to step back and set a long-term goal like, Over the next year, I will do some praying, thinking, counseling, and research on what God is calling me to do over the next five years.

What are my life dreams? We have been asking that question since we were in third grade, but now the asking gets serious because we are starting to realize that adult life is here. Answering this question should foster some healthy dreaming. Many contemporary youth leaders, however, are from the so-called baby-boom generation, and many of us in this generation have stopped dreaming. For a myriad of reasons, we are in danger of hanging on to the past, listening to oldies, and settling into mediocrity. I sometimes lose my dreams for fear of the future; at other times, I fail once and do not know how to dream again.

We desperately need new dreams in our lives. What would we like God to do uniquely through us? How do we desire our lives to affect the students we work with? In twenty years what do we dream of having done for God's kingdom? Dreams can get out of hand, however, especially if the human ego is substituted for a genuine desire to please God. But I grow more from dreaming big dreams and letting God remove the impurities than by not dreaming out of fear of mixed motives.

Dreaming is strategic because dreams help direct our efforts toward growth. If my dream is to see fifty alumni/ae of our youth ministry in full-time Christian service in twenty years, my dream pushes me to grow spiritually so that I can by personal example create a ministry environment that will encourage such a commitment in the students I lead.

Whom do I want to be like? Our choices of mentors and models likewise help us set growth goals for ourselves. When I read about the hours that Martin Luther or George Mueller spent in prayer, I reevaluate my own prayer life and make goals for long-term growth in that area. When I read about my friend Les Christie and his perseverance in youth ministry at the same church for over twenty years, it inspires me to ask myself how I can build love for people and faithfulness to the Lord so I can stay fresh in the same location for the long haul.

Mentors and models whether living or dead illustrate the character traits and spiritual growth that we would like for ourselves. Looking at their lives makes us step back and say: What quality do they exemplify that I would like to have? and How can I grow to be like them in that respect? From the answer to the second question come the goals that we can set for ourselves in our sustained growth.

How do I want to live? My long-term aspirations affect my spiritual choices and my ministry calling. More than a few have left youth ministry because their material aspirations could not be met on a youth leader's salary. Sadly, there are too many situations in which turnover is encouraged because the salary drives the youth leader who has a spouse and children into secular work or into other ministry positions that pay more.

The realities of underpaid youth workers notwithstanding, we still have to take a hard look at our lifestyles. At times I have realized that I was dissatisfied with a youth leader's pay because I had expectations for a lifestyle that was simply out of my reach. During these moments I have come to grips with greed, jealousy, and covetousness in myself, characteristic ingredients of our materialistic world, but destructive to my spiritual growth.

Asking ourselves hard questions about our lifestyle aspirations enables us to keep every area of our lives open before Jesus. We will be hampered in our spiritual growth if we aspire economically to the lifestyles of the rich and famous. If we live beyond our means (using the ubiquitous credit card) or strive for material success, we harm ourselves. Paul wrote to Timothy that "people who want to get rich fall into temptation and a trap and into many foolish and harmful desires that plunge men into ruin and destruction" (1 Tim. 6:9).

Asking ourselves about our lifestyle desires helps us maintain a long-term dedication to spiritual growth because it keeps us from being distracted, helps us distinguish need versus greed, and calls us to rededicate ourselves to the simpler life needed by followers of Jesus.

ON YOUR MARK,
GET SET . . .

Goal setting according to a long-term view of our lives brings us to the basics of day-to-day living. We need to ask, If these are my long-term dreams, how am I going to live *today*? I am a nuts-and-bolts type of person, so I like to conclude times of personal evaluation with some basic goal setting in light of my answers to the questions listed above. I start with the most practical (daily) and move to the long-term (yearly).

What spiritual-growth goal will I set for today? If I realize that I am neglecting prayer, I try to establish a remedial goal: Praying daily for ten minutes means taking out my calendar and blocking off the time. It also might mean a five-minute prayer time in immediate response to the goal, with the hope of reaching my goal by the end of the week. Remember that these goals are to perpetuate our growth, not to cause anxiety or unnecessary guilt. Today's goals are intended to be catalysts for growth, not a new list of legalistic bondage that makes us want to avoid time alone with God.

Daily goals in response to a long-term perspective usually apply to habits that we would like to develop over our lifetimes: Prayer, Scripture reading, writing in a journal, or quiet talks with our spouses might all fall into this category.

What spiritual-growth goal will I set this week? In a recent evaluation I found that I could not remember the last time I had memorized a verse from the Scriptures. Since I knew that I wanted to know the Bible well, I set a goal to pick and memorize one new verse over the next week. A weekly goal might include exercise, reading, study time, or outreach.

In light of my goal to be a motivator of others towards world missions, I know that I should be exemplifying outreach to non-Christians, the folks I desire to influence. Yet on looking at how I use my time, I find that church work often results in spending all of my time with Christians. Rather than overwhelming myself with a daily goal that I know I cannot reach, I set one that may be more possible to attain: This week my goal is to get out of the office at least once, pray for a chance to engage someone in conversation (which includes positioning myself in a location where I will meet new people), and initiate a conversation.

I tried this a week ago. While I did not get to share a full presentation of the gospel, I made an acquaintance with someone in town who is dabbling in the Rastafarian movement in Jamaica. I do not know what the encounter did for this man, but it challenged me to grow.

What spiritual-growth goal will I set this month? A half day in study, a block of time dedicated to prayer, or even an extra day off with my family may not be reachable today or this week, but I can set the goal to accomplish one of those goals over the next month. Looking at my time proactively, I can set aside hours each month for the offensive study I need or the extra preparation time I want to take for a special project. A monthly growth goal could include setting aside time to meet with an older Christian we admire for advice and counsel. It might include a one-day conference or a few hours to listen to a few of the tapes we have accumulated over the past six months.

What spiritual-growth goal will I set this year? Evaluation of long-term priorities takes time, so after I do an extensive one on myself, I immediately set a time twelve months in advance to do it again. This helps me set goals that are not only measurable, but also time-dated. The following are examples of yearly goals.

- To read through the New or Old Testament (or whole Bible, if possible).
- To attend a conference or continuing education course at a Christian school specifically for my own growth.
- To write to (or meet with) a mentor in my life for advice.

- To consult with two trusted leaders at my church for their candid critiques of my spiritual growth and my progress in ministry.

These samples show that year-long growth goals should be made in response to the question, "At the end of the next twelve months, where do I want to see spiritual growth in my life?"

Personal long-term evaluation leads to goal setting, but we need to keep it simple. I advocate a "do something once" approach, using the divisions listed above. If after a time of personal review I can walk away with a goal for each day, week, month, and year, it has been a *very* profitable day in projecting some direction to the immediate future.

A SQUASH
OR AN OAK?

Over-stressed youth leaders look at the concept of long-term goal setting with skepticism: "Sure, it's great for you, but I have no time for such noble concepts. I'm too busy just doing the basics of my ministry." My question is this: Are you willing to take a few hours of time to wrestle with issues that affect your entire life, or will you allow yourself to be eaten alive by the tyranny of the urgent?

A student asked the president of his school whether he could not take a shorter course than the one prescribed. "Oh yes," replied the president, "but then it depends upon what you want to be. When God wants to make an oak, He takes an hundred years, but when He wants to make a squash, He takes six months."[3]

What is your choice—a squash or an oak? A sprinter or a marathoner?

CHAPTER FOURTEEN
TEAMWORK: ENCOURAGING EACH OTHER

A few years ago I could not swim. I could dog paddle a little, enough to bluff my friends at the beach, but I really could not swim. I was afraid to put my face in the water, and I did not even know the basic crawl stroke. Then my wife Christie took me swimming. I hated swimming so much that the smell of the chlorine in the pool made me nauseous. I looked for excuses not to go. But she was patient and got me started . . . in the shallow end . . . blowing bubbles . . . kicking . . . floundering around. It was mortifying, but she taught me how to swim.

We started swimming lengths of the pool together. She swam eighteen, I could manage four. She moved up to forty, I broke double figures. She set her goal for a mile (seventy-two lengths); mine was to swim eighteen without drowning. In the learning-to-swim process, the key for me was Christie's *encouragement*. She came alongside and imparted courage to me so that I could grow.

> AXIOM: Long-term spiritual growth comes as a result of the dynamic give and take of encouragement from and toward others.

BUILDING EACH OTHER UP

In our ongoing desire for spiritual health and growth, we need people who will be committed to growing alongside of us. These are usually our coworkers in the youth ministry, although some find this type of encouragement in regional youth-leader associations or from friends outside the youth ministry. Growth through encouragement is a two-way street. There is a special accountability in relating to our superiors or our mentors, but here my focus is mutuality. As others encourage us to grow, we can likewise encourage them.

To find an encourager is one of the greatest benefits of teamwork in the body of Christ. Barnabas, also called the "Son of Encouragement" (Acts 4:36), came alongside of Paul to give him the support he needed when he was accepted into the church he had formerly persecuted. Similarly, Paul came alongside of timid Timothy to stir him to courage and action.

One of the words in the Scriptures that we translate "encourage" comes from the same root word as "comforter," used in reference to the Holy Spirit (John 14 and 16). It carries the connotation of one who comes alongside to help. The Holy Spirit comes alongside to encourage us, make us bold, give us a spiritual boost, and strengthen us to remain faithful to the Lord. He encourages by comforting; the two actions coincide. When we benefit from the ministry of encouragement, it is because one has come alongside another who is weak, fearful, discouraged, wavering in faith. By the Holy Spirit's power, we build each other up through this ministry of encouragement.

The writer of Hebrews exhorted his readers to have this kind of ministry toward each other in the face of hardships: "But encourage one another daily, as long as it is called Today, so that none of you may be hardened by sin's deceitfulness" (Heb. 3:13). Encouragement kept them soft in spirit and obedient to the Lord.

NO SMALL POTATOES

Encouragement and Christian growth go hand in hand, yet many of us become discouraged, overcome by spiritual malaise, or simply worn out. Why? Perhaps because the gift of encouragement that we need to give each other is so often neglected. We need someone to help us see progress.

Consider the ministry of encouragement that Christie exemplified when she was teaching me to swim.

Encouragement is pushy. Christian growth (like swimming) is supposed to be basic. We assume that everyone is doing it, yet many of us (like me doing the dog paddle) are just bluffing our way along. We need encouragement to get started, and this often includes a push, (what the Bible calls "spurring one another on to love and good deeds" (Heb. 10:24). In practical terms this might mean planning substantial time in our youth-leadership group for sharing, prayer, and even book study. (By "youth-leadership group" I mean a team of coworkers—usually volunteers—who assist in the leadership and discipleship of the youth ministry. These are the most valuable peers in the growth process because they know us, and they know the youth ministry. As such, they can be extraordinary encouragers to us.) It is unsafe to assume that everyone is growing.

Encouragement is honest. Christie could not teach me to swim until I acknowledged that I could not. Growth starts by recognizing that we are in need. An encourager loves us enough to help us see ourselves honestly, even with our failures. From this posture of honesty, we can start to make progress. It might be difficult for our entire youth-leadership team to accept our weaknesses, fears, or down times, but we can find within that group a peer or two who will pray with us, drop us a note, or give us a call when they recognize that we are limping spiritually.

Encouragement is verbal. If Christie was not reinforcing me with words like "You can do it" or "You're making progress," I surely would have quit. When we are feeling like failures in the Christian life, we need friends who come alongside and say, "You are forgiven by Christ; get back up and move on!"

Many of us feel discouraged because the only words we hear from other Christians (including parents and even our pastors) are, "You are falling short!" If we are honest before God, we know that we are sinners; we need words of encouragement to be assured that, even if we are not perfect, at least we're moving in the right direction.

How about this idea? Why not make it a regular practice to send notes of encouragement to each other on the leadership team? For us it has been a tremendous way of building teamwork and spreading encouragement.

Encouragement is exemplary. I persevered in my swimming lessons because I knew that Christie had put herself through the same grueling learning experience only a few years earlier. To encourage me she came alongside and said, "I did this, and so can you." If we lead others by example, we are far more likely to encourage them. The "do as I say, not as I do" style of leadership has no place in youth ministry.

Encouragement acknowledges progress. Christie never taunted me by reminding me of how many laps she was doing in contrast to my feeble efforts. Instead she always pointed out, "You went further today than you have ever gone before!" Words like these motivated me to go even further the next time. The greatest encouragers in my ministry have helped me by showing me how far I have come, not how far I have to go. All of us are encouraged by observable growth.

Encouragement is reciprocal. As Christie saw me improve as a novice swimmer, she was encouraged herself. She could see the effect her ministry of encouragement had on me, and this encouraged her. Believe it or not, our coworkers enjoy seeing our growth. It is humbling to have a fellow member of the leadership team affirm me with words like, "Paul, I am encouraged because I can see you are maturing." I need to take that encouragement as a genuine expression of his love for me and his desire to see God's best in my life.

Encouragement fosters growth. As a swimmer I now swim regularly far more than I would have ever thought possible. In the same way, when we are giving and receiving encouragement, we can grow into greater Christian maturity than we might have ever imagined.

WE NEED ALL
THE HELP WE CAN GET

Beyond our team of youth-ministry coworkers, spouses, and closest peers, we can also look for spiritual help from those we do not know personally—both the living and the dead. We can find help from the living in the following ways:

- *From reading.* One friend of mine referred to a favorite Christian author as a "Barnabas" to him. That author's books had consistently been used in my friend's life as a catalyst to his spiritual growth.
- *From asking questions.* Older, more experienced Christians can often offer the encouragement we need without even knowing it as they respond to our cries for help in the Christian life.
- *From other speakers, seminars, or training.* An urban youth worker heard me tell the story of Marilyn Laszlo (the Wycliffe Bible translator who had less than one good story per year) and approached me afterwards. "God had me here just to hear that story," he said. "I have been so close to quitting this month because I have seen so few results lately. That story motivated me to persevere."

We can also find spiritual help from the dead. When I feel like a spiritual failure, I enjoy reading the book of Judges. As I look at indecisive Gideon, sinful Samson, or some of the others highlighted in this book, I remember that if God worked through *them*, he can certainly use me! The biblical narratives and special passages like Hebrews 11 can give us a shove forward.

Reading Christian history can also help. Although there were no youth workers per se before the Industrial Age, I still find great encouragement in reading about the impact that God had on others' lives through his imperfect saints. Ruth Tucker's book *From Jerusalem To Irian Jaya* summarizes God's work through people over the past two thousand years in pithy, two-to five-page excerpts (she even has an index on such topics as loneliness or hardship to direct me to the most helpful biographical sketches).

FINDING THE RIGHT KIND OF HELP

As we look within our coterie of friends or to other men and women in Christian leadership (dead or alive) for help in maintaining spiritual growth, what are we after?

First, we should look for *models of godliness*. The best help we can get in the Christian journey comes from those who are a little further along in their walk with Christ. On our youth team I try to recruit at least a few older people who have been Christians for a few decades. These men and women might not be the most effective with students, but they serve as a great encouragement to the rest of the youth-leadership team in godliness.

Second, we should look for *models of love*. Two youth workers at an international conference inspired me to love the people God had sent me to. One was returning to serve in a youth ministry in Beirut, Lebanon. The other was returning to his home in Colombo, Sri Lanka. Both men and their families faced uncertainty, hardship, and possibly death. I asked them why they were returning. They responded, "Because we love our people; since they have no choice but to stay, we will stay with them." As I contemplated their example, I repented of my own coldness and impatience towards my people.

Third, we should look for *models of mercy*. Encouragement is often believing the best in people, even when the people have not earned the right to be believed. The biblical example of Barnabas with Mark speaks of mercy, and Barnabas' example reminds me of God's mercy towards me; it encourages me to press on.

Finally, we should look for *models of faithfulness*. As we look for encouragement to press on in the faith, we are stimulated by those who pressed on before us. When I went through seminary, I often wondered if I should persevere; What is this worth? I asked myself. God used my classmates Jack and Ron, veteran youth workers with over fifty years experience between them, to spur me on. Their hunger to learn, to grow, and to stretch their minds encouraged me to do the same.

HELP WANTED: ENCOURAGERS

On the coldest days of our northern winters, we often find that our car battery has lost its charge during the night. The engine will not turn over because the battery is too weak. The ministry of encouragement is like the car that comes alongside ours and gives us a jump start. The strength of the operative car is transferred to the dead battery, and the inoperative car is rejuvenated to action.

When we are discouraged, saddened by the hardships of life, or simply tired of the Christian path of obedience, we need coworkers who will come alongside us and give us a spiritual jump start. As Christ and other members of the body of Christ strengthen us, we can strengthen others. By God's Holy Spirit, we can assist each other to live the Christian life.

God gives us partners in the ministry of encouragement who, by the power of the Holy Spirit, help us press on in the upward challenge of spiritual growth. As they encourage us they strengthen us to encourage others, thus building the body of Christ.

And let us consider how we spur one another on toward love and good deeds. Let us not give up meeting together, as some are in the habit of doing, but let us *encourage one another*—and all the more as you see the Day approaching (Heb. 10:24-25).

CHAPTER FIFTEEN
PERSPECTIVE: TIME ALONE WITH GOD

Busyness. Christie and I recognized it as our common enemy. As we came to the end of a long stretch when I had been away (retreats, a conference, a study day) for the better part of three weeks, and she had been preparing for exams and writing two papers, we awkwardly came together for a quiet evening alone. We needed to get reacquainted, and we did not know where to start.

Relationships take time. It is a basic rule that applies to all of us, and when we approach our spiritual health and growth, we come face to face with our relationship with God. We often come to him after weeks or days of busyness, and like my wife and me, we sense an awkwardness and distance because of the gap in time since our last meeting.

> AXIOM: Spiritual health is a direct result of time spent with God. The long-term growth we achieve will be built on the cultivation of this primary relationship.

WHY THE DISTANCE?

I have made all sorts of excuses in my life for not taking time to come into God's presence to worship, listen, or learn. Busyness is only one excuse. There is *fear* (that I have done something wrong and would rather not hear about it), *doubt* (that God really desires me to come), *fatigue* (if I get on my knees and bury my face in the bed, I may not wake up for hours), and *procrastination* (tomorrow I will have more time to devote), to name only a few. Most of my excuses pale by comparison to the overwhelming benefits of time spent in the presence of Christ!

Time alone with God helps us look like Jesus. The basic principle underlying 1 John 3:2—that we shall be like Christ because we shall see him as he is—is that seeing Christ as he is helps us become more like him. C.S. Lewis illustrated the Christian life as "dressing up like Jesus" until we eventually begin to look like him. The apostles in Acts 4:13 were recognized as having been with Jesus. Perhaps the greatest mark of growth we can ever aspire to is to be recognized as having been with Jesus.

My maternal grandparents had a courtship that lasted seven years prior to their fifty-four-year marriage. When my grandfather died, the two of them actually looked like each other. There was no blood relationship, but sixty-one years together had affected their language, their facial mannerisms, and even their physical appearance. Transformed means to be changed in character. If people can transform each other through time together, how much more can the Lord change us through time with him?

Time alone with God puts our lives in perspective. When I am under pressure, I worry. I worry about things going wrong; I worry about missing deadlines; I worry about forgetting something. Even after trying to walk with Jesus for almost twenty years, I worry. If I can repress my anxiety, my dreams often tell me what is going on inside.

On my first opportunity to preach at Grace Chapel, I compensated for my anxiety by a massive amount of study and preparation. I rehearsed the sermon to an empty sanctuary, and I preached it to Christie three times. The night before I preached, I dreamt that I walked into the pulpit to preach, but I had forgotten my pants! My dream told me that inside I was still feeling unprepared. Perhaps I should have spent more time preparing my spirit before God!

As someone who is prone to blow responsibilities, issues, failures, and successes out of proportion, I have learned the absolute necessity of time alone with God. To prevent myself from either wallowing in my faults or becoming self-satisfied with my successes, I need God's perspective. I need to be still and know that he is God (Psa. 46:10) and in control of my life. It is the best way to keep from overreacting to crises or becoming too concerned with matters over which I have no control.

Time in God's presence puts my life back in order. This was Job's lesson. He pleaded his innocence before God as a reason for an explanation for his sufferings. Then God reoriented Job's perspective with, "Where were you?" (chapters 38 and following). When Job saw the Almighty God, he was reduced to true repentance. His perspective on himself, the world, and God was changed.

When we are beaten down by life's circumstances or unusually elevated by applause, we need time in God's presence so that our perspectives are stabilized. Devotional writer F.B. Meyer put it this way.

> God puts us where He wants us. God seeks to mold us by our circumstances, and you must believe that God has put you just where you are because your present position is the very best place in the universe to make you what He wants you to become.
>
> You may be a clerk, a cook, a housemaid, but God had the whole universe to choose from, and He wanted to do His best for you. He put your soul just where it is because He knew that there you would be surrounded by the best conditions to make you what He wanted you to become. (source unknown)

Time with God does not always show us why God put us in a certain situation, but it assures us that he is at work through that situation.

Time alone with God shines his light on our lives. The greatest discomfort of spiritual growth is conviction. We would rather stay in the grey twilight than have the full light of the sun beating down on us. In the spiritual twilight, our impurities can stay hidden, but in the full light of God's revelation, we see ourselves as we really are.

In *Back to the Heart of Youth Work*, veteran youth leader Dewey Bertolini points out that we have too often fallen prey to the temptation of measuring youth-ministry leadership based on "communication skill, vision, enthusiasm, organizational ability, personality, gifts, or raw guts."[1] In contrast, he says we need to be reminded of "the single most essential ingredient needed for being useful to the Master—personal purity."[2]

Rereading questions about sexual temptation is enough to convince me that I do not want to go into God's presence today. When I think of this area and every other area in which I sin by thought or deed, I fear spending time alone with God. Then I remember forgiveness; then I remember the returning prodigal son and his father's response.

We all fear having our motives, thoughts, and actions measured against the standards of a holy God, but only as we come into his presence do we find the true measure of God's love for us. He removes our transgressions from us as far as the East is from the West, and through Jesus he welcomes us with merciful open arms (Psa. 103:10-14).

Time alone with God quiets our hearts. Jesus sets the example in Mark 1:35. He was in the habit of slipping away early in the day to worship and pray. Later in Jesus' life, after the death of John the Baptist reminded Jesus of the future that awaited him, he encouraged his disciples to join him in getting away to a quiet place where they could rest (Mark 6:31).

The Quakers taught the discipline of "centering down." By releasing the external cares that surround us and focusing on the Lord as the center and sustainer of our lives, we can find his strength in our weakness and his peace in the midst of our storms. All of us benefit from refocusing our attention on God as the center of our being, our lives, and our ministries. When I am frantic with anxiety, stressed by pressure, and feeling overworked and underappreciated, I must quiet down and realize that it is God, not I, who holds my life together. I choose a time to center down with the simple prayer, "Lord Jesus, please bring order to my life."

Time alone with God equips us for ministry. When we look over all of the jobs and expectations associated with youth ministry, we inevitably respond with the apostle Paul, "Who is equal to such a task?" (2 Cor. 2:16). Time spent in God's presence reminds us that our adequacy rests in Christ alone.

Dewey Bertolini cites ten biblical mandates basic to the position of pastor and applies them to the youth leader. The youth pastor must: (1) guard the flock (Acts 20:28); (2) feed the flock (Acts 20:28); (3) oversee the flock (Acts 20:28); (4) agonize over the flock (Acts 20:31); (5) know the flock (John 10:3); (6) equip the flock (Col. 1:28); (7) reprove, rebuke, exhort the flock (2 Tim. 4:2); (8) tenderly love the flock (1 Thess. 2:7); (9) evangelize (2 Tim. 4:5); and (10) endure severe reactions (2 Tim. 4:3).[3]

An overwhelming list to be sure! But I have found too often that when I read a list like that, I set about trying to make myself more equipped for the task. I try reading more, caring more, and serving more until I burn myself out. Then I come back to realize that God may eventually direct me to read, care, and serve, but I must *first* come to him, realizing that my efforts are futile without his power.

Time alone with God helps us prioritize. When my eyes go out of focus, I get headaches, I feel nauseous, and my ability to work effectively suffers. The same is true of our lives. When we scatter our efforts, we get "headaches" from overwork, and an "upset stomach" because we are not really sure what difference our efforts will make, and our work suffers. We need focus. To understand a personal life goal or any sense of what God wants us uniquely to do, we need a focus. Time spent with God helps us see his call on our lives and how we can spend our energies for maximum effectiveness.

When I was first asked to do youth ministry at our church, my father strongly advised against it. He said that I was too heavy into discipleship for work with teens. But time alone with God told me otherwise. God directed me to my "heavy" strengths to disciple young people, and he called out a cooperative team of people to work with me. They served to complement me. As a result, I could use my gifts of challenging and exhorting to maximum effectiveness.

BACK TO THE BASICS

We would all like to be established in the day-to-day discipline of prayer, reflection, and Scripture reading, but how do we do it? What are our realistic goals? And what tools might help us build this discipline of time alone with God?

Several years ago I found a booklet by Lorne Sanny, then the president of the Navigators, an organization committed to discipleship. The title intrigued me: *How To Spend a Day in Prayer*. Since I was interested in growing spiritually, and spending a day in prayer seemed like a spiritual thing to do, I bought the booklet. I looked over my calendar and found a day that I could block off to spend the whole day in prayer. I anticipated the day, reading and rereading the booklet so I would know what to do. Just the thought of spending a whole day in prayer was already making me more spiritual. (I confided in several others about my plan, and they looked at me with a "day in prayer today, water into wine tomorrow" admiration.)

The day came. With booklet, Bible, and journal in hand, I went off into the woods. The first two hours went quite well. Reading, writing, thinking, and praying filled the time. It seemed like the time was flying by until I looked at my watch. My spirituality was broken for a fleeting moment as I thought to myself, What the heck am I going to do for the next six hours? But I tried more reading, writing, thinking, and praying.

By noon my mind wandered to lunch—that is, what other people were having for lunch, since I had decided to go the full spiritual course by fasting, too. The booklet helped give me some new ideas of things to pray about, but I could not find anything about resisting mosquitoes in the booklet, and my attention span was waning as the bugs increased. At about three o'clock, I came out of the woods, hoping that no one would see me. Those I had boasted to would surely be expecting me to have a Moses-like glow about my face, and all I had were mosquito bites.

My experience taught me a valuable lesson: Time spent alone with God in prayer and meditation is like any exercise—the stronger we get, the more we can do. The corollary is also true: I should not expect to jump to spending a day in prayer if I currently consider thirty to sixty minutes my spiritual maximum.

BABY STEPS

The best way to build up to a day in prayer is to take it gradually. This week I would like to increase my quiet times with God to thirty minutes a day. Over the next month, perhaps I can see myself setting aside one three-hour block to join others in a Concert of Prayer.[4] Within the next six months, maybe I could get a friend to go away with me for a half-day session of prayer and meditative reading. Given my present spiritual state, perhaps I could think about a day in quietness and prayer next year at this time.

One of my friends takes a full day for prayer and study every month, and he adds to it a silent retreat (seven days of silent reflection without talking to anyone but God) every year. He would probably spurn my advice, complaining that I was not challenging people to go further and faster in their time alone with God. He may be correct, but I would rather encourage gradually growing toward a day in prayer than diving into it immediately only to return home defeated.

TOOL KIT

It may sound impersonal or mechanical to think of our relationship with God in terms of setting goals or using tools, but they are only suggested to serve as thrusters, pushing us in the right direction. Obviously, the Bible is key to helping us get to know God and spend time in his presence. "Any leader who fails to take nourishment daily from the Word of God will most certainly degenerate into a voice from a vacuum."[5] A journal or personal prayer diary is also useful. Journaling our thoughts and prayers or using a daily devotional guide like Oswald Chambers' *My Utmost For His Highest* or John Baillie's *Diary of Private Prayer* can help stimulate our meditations.

Another tool to consider is the location of our personal time with God. A.W. Tozer had the ability to concentrate even in a mob, to the point where ideas for his classic book *The Knowledge of the Holy* may have been generated while commuting to work on the bus. But most of us need more quiet than that. An empty office after hours may be a good spot, or a spot outdoors, weather permitting, may suit us best (bring mosquito repellent if you are headed for the New Hampshire woods). I do best with a comfortable, quiet location—preferably the same spot every day.

Time of day should be looked at as well. I am a morning person, so I prefer the early hours before breakfast. If I wait until the end of the day, I usually doze off. A friend tells me that he does not even start to wake up until 4:00 p.m., and at midnight he is just hitting full stride. Whatever our metabolism, we do best to offer to God the time of day when we are most alert. Music soothes the spirit and can be an effective tool during time alone with God—especially to drown out background noise. Tapes of praise songs or Scriptures set to music can guide us in personal times of worship.

Finally, I recommend a pad of paper nearby to write down ideas that come during quiet moments. Inevitably, just as I am getting quiet before God, three thoughts spring into my mind— details about the upcoming banquet, students I need to call, or brainstorms about next week's Bible study. Rather than trying to repress these business details, I prefer to write them down on a pad of paper so that I do not have to think about them until my time of personal worship is over.

BEATING THE CURSE OF SHALLOWNESS

Superficiality is the curse of our age. We become superficial because we fill our lives with busyness at the expense of our relationship with God. Since the cultivation of spiritual depth takes time, we need to put time alone with God high on our priority list. Without time in his presence for worship, listening, and learning, our other efforts toward spiritual growth will be in vain.

CHAPTER SIXTEEN
GETTING AWAY: ENLARGING MY PERSPECTIVE

A Boston travel agency tries to attract customers to its office with the clever phrase, "Please—Go Away." As we contemplate building for long-term spiritual health, I advise the same— "Please, go away." Getting away by means of a conference, a seminar, a day in prayer, or a personal vacation—has been one of the greatest sustainers to my own personal growth. Through periodic times away from the church and ministry, I have been able to clear the muddle from my head, gain a fresh perspective on myself and my ministry, and recommit myself to spiritual growth.

Responses to the getting-away principle vary widely. Most agree with the concept, but a few of us bemoan our economic hardships or the demands on our time. Getting away seems impossible. On the other end of the spectrum are the youth leaders who oppose the getting-away principle as being unspiritual and unnecessary. One group boasts, "I would rather burn out than rust out." Another responds, "The Devil *never* takes a vacation. Why should I?"

Burning out for Jesus sounds like a noble desire, but it seems to me that long-term perseverance in his service might do far more good. Neither burning out nor rusting out sounds too desirable. I would rather last.

Whether or not the Devil takes a vacation, I do not know. I do know this: The Devil is not our mentor! Perhaps the Devil never takes a vacation, but who wants to imitate the Devil? We follow the God who rested on the seventh day of creation, and the Lord who told his followers, "Come with me by yourselves to a quiet place and get some rest" (Mark 6:31).

> **AXIOM:** The biblical principle of the Sabbath means that we need time away from our ministries and normal routines to engage in reflection that allows us to be spiritually refreshed to continue.

NURTURING OUR PERSONAL GROWTH

Taking a break away from our day-to-day routines can help us get back on the growth track. Sometimes we get so caught up in responsibilities that we stop thinking. We need to get away— for an hour, a day, a few days, or even a week. We know that getting away is biblical. Jesus set the example by frequent departures from the crowds to be alone with God in prayer. We also know (from the advice of others as well as our own experiences) that time away gives us perspective on ourselves and our ministries. When we look at the way we are spending our time, and we have no answer to the question, "Why am I doing this?" we need a break.

We need time away for physical rest as well. The interaction of our physical state and our spiritual well-being is fairly easy to demonstrate. The more tired we are, the shorter our tempers, and the greater our likelihood for poor decisions. When my spirit and body are exhausted, I have greater difficulty loving the needy person and persevering with the family that seems to be making no progress.

BUT HOW?

The demands and realities of the youth worker's schedule make carrying out get-away time difficult, but all of us need to get out of the daily routine to take some spiritual inventory in our lives.

Here are some practical ideas that have helped me to stay fresh.

Take our day off, off. Time with family, a walk in the woods, or shopping in the city might provide a refreshing break on given days. Extra time in a study or time just to watch a movie can all be part of a day off. The greatest struggle I have faced is disciplining myself not to work on this day. An unwillingness to let go of my work for a day hurts me, my relationship with my wife, and my chances of spiritual refreshment with God.

How we use our days off can vary widely. One couple loves to spend the day with adult peers who are not involved in the youth ministry. My wife and I prefer to be alone. Unmarried leaders might prefer doing something relaxing with youth-ministry peers (without discussing business) or with friends outside the youth ministry. Taking off one day a week helps me to get rested physically and refreshed spiritually. In addition, it reminds me in a healthy way that I am expendable. The person who insists, "I simply cannot take a day off—the work is too important," is either trying to accomplish too much or has an exaggerated idea of his or her own importance.

Hot tip: Christie has worked outside the home since we were married, so we have had to work hard to try to get one day off a week *together*. We do not always succeed, but we have found that we succeed more when we sit down with our calendars and mark "day off" for the next three months. It might sound mechanical, but we find that it works. With me in the ministry and both of us working outside the home, spontaneity must be planned.

Take a vacation. Almost every job allows at least one week of vacation a year, and we need to take that time to be away from the ministry. Here is where economic issues surface, especially for married youth workers with young families. Since Christie and I both work and have no children, we have struggled to get our schedules to coincide, but we have not had to struggle too much with economics.

For those who think vacations are not possible due to finances, consider several alternatives. Dan, Mary, and their children refused to take a vacation one year because they had nowhere to go (due to money). Since that week at home was not restful (and people from church still dropped by), they decided that the next year they would try camping. The next Christmas they exchanged gifts of camping equipment, and the next summer they took off to an inexpensive campground. It was hardly a luxurious vacation, but they enjoyed the time away as a family.

Tom, Kim, and their kids decided to accept an offer from a family in the church to use their vacation home. At first they were nervous that the family was offering a favor to gain a favor, but they were pleasantly surprised. The family was simply being generous, and Tom, Kim and family got a vacation they desperately needed.

Some youth workers speak at summer camps in exchange for a vacation option for their families. While this involves some ministry, it can still be refreshing, especially if all of the speaking is in the evening and the youth worker can use messages that were already prepared from a previous retreat or camp.

For most of us in youth ministry, neither time nor money will allow for a perfect vacation, but the benefits of getting away together make even a not-so-perfect vacation well worthwhile.

Hot tip: For maximum spiritual refreshment on a vacation, I take only a Bible, a journal, and one or two books for spiritual stimulation. When we went on our first vacations, I took eight to ten books from my to-read shelf, and I found that I either felt guilty for ignoring them on vacation or I ignored my vacation while I caught up on reading. I have found that time to think and evaluate spiritual growth is more valuable than checking eight books off my list.

Take a speaking engagement. If our employing church or organization will allow it, time away to minister to others can be quite refreshing, if we plan for it. Ministering effectively to someone else's youth group (even using material that might have been received coldly in our own ministry) can reassure us that God does use us in the lives of others. An outside trip can give us the appreciation we need to return home to serve those who sometimes take us for granted.

An outside ministry opportunity helps me to grow when I use the driving time for extra prayer. If I am alone, I can use my free time for special reading or thinking about our ministry at home. Time in flight or in the airport can be useful for reading, and time with my host can provide an education experience when I ask questions about his or her personal growth in the face of youth ministry demands.

Hot tip: Ask the question, "What can I learn from my host, the time away, and the topic I am asked to speak about?" before accepting a speaking engagement. Rather than seeing outside speaking opportunities as merely extra ministry or a chance to earn a few extra dollars, we can make them part of our continuing education in ministry.

Take in a conference. Each year we plan into our respective budgets a few hundred dollars for professional growth. This is our way of saying that we value a ministry-related conference. Instead of overloading myself with input at conferences (like I used to), I now choose a simpler route. I try to pace myself by choosing speakers, workshops, and seminars wisely. Time alone in my hotel room to think through a particularly challenging workshop is more valuable to me than rushing off to attend another one.

Conferences can also lose their value if we allow the time away to be dominated by concerns at home. It is probably wise to call and check in every other day, but when I meet someone who is calling the church office two to three times a day, I wonder if he would have been wiser to have stayed home.

In a similar way, I think a conference loses its potential benefit if I spend a majority of my one-on-one conversations complaining about my present pastor or my work situation. I used to find great comfort in participating in "can you top this?" complaint sessions about the church, but I now prefer to leave a conference with a few positive ideas rather than simply find the "fellowship of suffering" with those whose ministry seems as bad as or worse than mine.

Hot tip: When I go to a conference, I think in terms of ones. Who is *one* person with whom I can meet to ask questions and get advice? Is there *one* book I can buy, *one* seminar I can attend, or *one* speaker I must hear to encourage my growth? Can I make *one* friendship (perhaps someone I can correspond with) for mutual accountability and growth? What is *one* idea I can take with me to apply to my personal growth and/or ministry?

THE PAUSE
THAT REFRESHES

Time away allows us to get outside the routine and above the details so that we can return with a refreshed perspective. As a youth leader, I have even used time away on short-term mission service teams as an opportunity for special growth. While there are a myriad of details, the routine is different, the work is different, and there is usually more time for Bible study and personal prayer. These times have enabled me to return to the ministry stronger than when I left.

When we feel exhausted, spiritually fatigued, or drying up in our ability to care for others ... please, go away! If Almighty God rested and was refreshed on the Sabbath day of Creation, should we not follow his example?

CHAPTER SEVENTEEN
ACCOUNTABILITY: WHO IS KEEPING ME HONEST?

"I hope that the choice you have made in mentors turns out better than the choices I made," I said to Jimmy and Tim, two men who were looking to me as a spiritual example. We were talking about two of my spiritual mentors, who were now out of the ministry because of sinful moral choices.

"Whether we made the right choice or not," Jimmy responded, "is up to you!"

Jimmy reminded me that my example before them was still my responsibility. My choices included making wise decisions with my own life so that I could avoid the falls of the men who preceded me. As I evaluated the lives of my former mentors, I realized that both men had been living in isolation. It seemed that they had no peers, and I wondered if anyone, even their spouses, knew what was going on in their hearts. After seeing their fall and being reminded of my responsibility to Jimmy, Tim, and others, I decided I needed an accountability partner, someone who would ask me hard questions, keep me from bluffing, and hold my feet to the fire concerning my spiritual growth.

AXIOM: Spiritual health demands a friend who will walk alongside us, speak truth to us (even when it hurts), and keep us honest in our relationship with God and with other people.

HURTS
SO GOOD

An accountability partner is someone who loves us enough to wound. Rather than letting us wander down the road of self-deception, they give us a slap in the face that demands our attention. "Better is open rebuke than hidden love. Wounds from a friend can be trusted, but an enemy multiplies kisses" (Prov. 27:5-6). Richard served this role in my life several years ago. As we sat in a college cafeteria one day, he interrupted our conversation with a confrontation. "Paul, I have noticed that every time a young woman goes by your eyes scan up and down her body. Where is your mind wandering?"

I wanted to react defensively. I felt angry and hurt that my friend would accuse me of lustful thinking. I desired to lash back with, "And what makes you so holy?" But I had nothing to say. Richard loved me enough to wound me. Together we had agreed to "spur one another on toward love and good deeds" (Heb. 10:24), and he was merely stirring me up in an area that he saw needed work.

The older we get as Christians, the better we get at spiritual charades. We need someone who will ask penetrating questions to reveal our spiritual state and then love us enough to help us grow. Norm and I get together with our wives every two or three months. He is not a consistent accountability partner, but whenever we are together, he asks, "So, buddy, are you spending time with God each day?" On some occasions, knowing that Norm's question would come, I have prepared ahead of time so that I have a good answer. I hate being caught off guard. His question illustrates the benefits of accountability partners. To know that he was going to confront me motivated me to action. In the same way, having peers who will ask me questions about my growth, my thoughts, my reading, or my attitudes motivates me to positive action.

An accountability partner helps us not only by confrontation but also by affirmation. Earl Palmer describes a mentor as "someone who encourages you and keeps you going. A mentor builds up your confidence in your ability to think your own thoughts and make your own decisions."[1]

CALLING ALL ACCOUNTABILITY PARTNERS

Who can be an accountability partner to me? Can it be my spouse? A coworker at the church? How about the senior pastor? The accountability partner can be just about any fellow Christian who is committed unreservedly to tearing us down and building us up. The accountability partner should be someone who loves us, but not one who glosses over our flaws and failures. He or she should be someone who is willing to rebuke us to foster our growth, but not to destroy us.

I have always tried to have this kind of relationship with my wife, Christie, but I go beyond her to at least one male peer. In light of her love for me, I fear that she may not be as harsh on me as I sometimes need. Because of our male/female difference in perspectives, I need a male peer who will understand and rebuke me in areas of sexual temptation that Christie may not fully identify with. Earl Palmer writes (again using the term "mentor" for what I am calling an accountability partner) that this person "will likely be someone outside your church with whom you can meet regularly to talk about your work. Age does not matter—your mentor may be older than you, or a peer, or even a group of peers. You may be mutual mentors to each other by showing each other what you're writing [in a journal] and telling each other what you're thinking. However we find our mentor, we all need someone whose caring support and nonjudgmental listening helps us keep unlocking our gifts."[2]

KEEPING GOOD ACCOUNTS

In my current accountability relationship with Doug, we concentrate on asking each other questions, praying together, and reading to stimulate our thinking about ministry and growth. We have read books related to issues in ministry (*Power Evangelism*), classics (*Mere Christianity*), novels that we think will help us gain better understanding of our world (*Bonfire of the Vanities*), and thought-provoking theological works (*Foolishness to the Greeks*). The best part of our weekly get-togethers (usually ninety minutes) is not the reading, however, but rather the discussions about personal issues. How are our marriages growing? Where do we need help? What do we do when we see ourselves stagnating? How do we deal with sexual temptations when we travel?

Some people find this type of accountability in one-on-one relationships as I do. Others prefer small-group interaction in covenant groups. These groups usually agree to meet together for a set period of time each month or each week for a given duration (nine months to a year is usually the minimum). Whether in small groups or in one-on-one relationships, certain qualities characterize effective accountability relationships:

- *Honesty*—no bluffing or putting on our best face.
- *Love*—nothing we say will cause the other person to reject us.
- *Forgiveness*—the relationships illustrate to us the mercy of Jesus.
- *Questions*—we take initiative to ask each other about personal matters like devotional life, family life, ministry, attitudes, thoughts, and aspirations.
- *Counsel*—we give and take advice from each other without defensiveness; we say to each other, in effect, "Help me to grow," and then we agree to listen.

- *Confidentiality*—others will not be informed of the issues we share without our consent.
- *Commitment*—we are committed to regular meetings as a means of building mutual trust.

LOOKING AFTER NUMBER ONE

David Stone encourages the pursuit of a spiritual friend, someone with whom we can be vulnerable and from whom we can expect questions regarding our spiritual progress.[3] Bob has become such a man in my life. Recently I met with him at his request. We chatted for a few minutes, and then I asked him what was on his mind.

"I would like to meet with you regularly so that you can hold me accountable," he replied.

"What do you mean by that?" I asked.

Bob answered, "When we get together, I would like you to ask me, 'How is your number one?' because this will force me to evaluate who or what has been the top priority in my life over the last month, whether this is a proper godly priority, and what remedial action I need to take."

So now we meet regularly, and every time I ask him about his number one, I am forced to evaluate my own life.

CONCLUSION
SETTING THE PACE FOR GROWTH

Mark Twain described the Platte River as "a mile wide and a foot deep." I have often wondered if my own life could be described that way as I have tried to broaden my ministry without deepening my spiritual life. The antidote to shallowness is an aggressive approach to growth. When we are growing, we will be fresh for ministry and more likely to stimulate growth in others we touch. David Stone challenges us that "a spirituality program for your group depends on your own spirituality. If you do not have a spiritual growth program, how can you expect the youth in your ministry to grow spiritually? . . . The bottom line: The genesis of anything that really works is at the top. *Spiritual growth in youth ministry begins with you*" (emphasis mine).[1]

STAYING IN THE RACE

The hurdles of youth ministry are difficult. The exercises of spiritual discipline demand our total effort. We dedicate our lives to the ongoing process of being built up until we attain spiritual maturity. In the face of these awesome challenges, how do we stay in the race? What keeps us moving ahead?

Look back every once in awhile to see progress. This book might tend to discourage us with the challenges ahead. Rather than feeling overburdened with all of the areas I have yet to grow in (of which there are many!), I find consolation when I pause and look back to how far I have come. I may not yet be "perfect in Christ" (Col. 1:28), but I am further along than I was last year at this time.

Set a pace that can be sustained. I am not much of a runner, but I do know my limitations. If I am doing hundred-yard sprints, I run at one pace. If I am aiming for two miles, I run at quite another. I cannot possibly keep up in the sprinting pace for the longer run.

In the same way, we need to start where we are and set a pace for growth. Ultimate spirituality is not based on rapid growth (a sprinter's pace), but on consistent growth. I know that I would like to grow as fast as others seem to, but their pace is not my pace. I must set a pace with Jesus that helps me grow day after day, week after week, year after year.

Keep our eyes on Jesus. The Bible alludes to the Christian life as a race as well, and if we are to endure this race, we need to keep our eyes on Jesus (Heb. 12:1-2). As the mechanical rabbit stimulates the greyhounds to race, the example of Jesus set before us motivates us to endure life's long run.

A short while ago, our church held an appreciation night in my honor. Students stepped forward with kind words about the impact of the youth ministry. We partied and ate. After that evening I thought to myself, Perhaps now I will get some thank you notes from students and parents. After several weeks, I had received only three notes. I suppose I felt some self-pity, until I remembered words of Oswald Chambers in *My Utmost For His Highest*. He wrote that the Christian's determination to serve must never be based on our love for people, but on Christ's love for us. When we realize that Jesus loved us in the face of our rebellion and sin, we find in him the ability to love people the same way.

If my determination to serve were based on concrete results like thank you notes, my motivation to persevere would be dashed. But my job is to keep my eyes on Jesus and, by his grace, to keep going forward in the spiritual race.

WARNING: Veteran youth workers have determined that the side effects of youth work can be hazardous to your spiritual health.

The warning still holds for all of us—myself most of all. But by identifying the hurdles and working towards long-term solutions, we don't have to despair. We can develop and maintain spiritual health and maturity. More to the point, we must. God bless you as you journey.

ENDNOTES

Chapter One Motivation: What's Driving Me?

1. Les Steele, "Escape the Performance Trap," *Campus Life* (October 1988): LG15.
2. John Sanford, *Ministry Burnout* (New York: Paulist Press, 1982), 21.
3. Tony Campolo, "Hidden Reasons Behind the Revolving Door Syndrome," *Youthworker Journal* (Summer 1984): 24.
4. Ibid., 26.
5. Stephen R. Covey, *The Seven Habits of Highly Effective People* (New York: Simon and Schuster, 1989), 292-294.

Chapter Two Success: What Am I Striving for?

1. Robert S. McGee, *The Search for Significance* (Houston: Rapha Publishing, 1987), 34.
2. Cliff Harris, quoted in Tom Callahan, "Life's Not a Bowl of Any Single Thing," *Time* (January 27, 1986): 53.
3. Kent Keller, "How (Not) to Burn Out of Youth Ministry," *Campus Life* (January 1988): LG15.
4. Buster Soaries, "Who Are We Really?" *Campus Life* (December 1988): LG15.

Chapter Four The Learning Plateau: Have I Stagnated?

1. J. Robert Clinton, *The Making of a Leader* (Colorado Springs: NavPress, 1988), 114.

2. Ibid., 234.
3. Gail MacDonald, *Keep Climbing* (Wheaton: Tyndale, 1989), 121-125.
4. Mark Senter, "Five Stages in Your Ministry Development," *Leadership* (Spring 1989): 93.
5. Vance Havner, *The Best of Vance Havner* (Grand Rapids: Baker, 1969), 92-94.

Chapter Five Lust: Am I Waging the War Within?

1. Earl Palmer, "Safeguards Against Temptation," *Campus Life* (November 1988): LG15.

Chapter Six Busyness: Can I Fulfill Multiple Expectations?

1. Gail MacDonald, *Keep Climbing*. (Wheaton: Tyndale House, 1989), 30.

Section Two

1. Gordon MacDonald's book *Ordering Your Private World* (Nashville: Nelson, 1984) has been inspirational for many, but others have found the concept frustrating because of the impression that the state of having one's "private world" fully ordered is achievable. Like Thomas a Kempis' *Imitation of Christ*, the title should be seen as a challenge towards a good goal rather than a promise of full achievability.
2. Roberta Hestenes, interviewed in "Can Spirituality Be Taught?" *Leadership* (Fall 1988): 16.

Chapter Seven Forgiveness: Learning To Let Go of Failure

1. *The Book of Common Prayer* (New York: Oxford University Press, 1929), 6.
2. Donald McCullough, *Waking From the American Dream* (Downers Grove, Illinois: InterVarsity Press, 1987), 176.

3. J.I. Packer, *Knowing God* (Downers Grove, Illinois: Inter-Varsity Press, 1973), 115.

Chapter Eight Spiritual Disciplines: Spiritual Growth Does not Just Happen

1. Charles H. Spurgeon, quoted in Richard Ellsworth Day, *The Shadow of the Broad Brim* (Philadelphia: Judson, 1934), 131.
2. John R.W. Stott, *The Preacher's Portrait* (Grand Rapids: Eerdmans, 1961), 30.
3. Eugene Peterson, "Growth: An Act of the Will?" *Leadership* (Fall 1988): 34-40.

Chapter Nine Learning: Breaking Out of My Stagnation

1. Earl Palmer, "The Mind Alive," *Leadership* (Fall 1988): 86-89.
2. J. Robert Clinton, *The Making of a Leader* (Colorado Springs: NavPress, 1988), 180.
3. Palmer, *op. cit.*, 86.
4. Sammy Tippit, *The Prayer Factor* (Chicago: Moody Press, 1988), 41.
5. Paul Tournier, *The Strong and the Weak* (New York: Harper & Row, 1964).
6. Palmer, *op. cit.*, 87.

Chapter Ten Balance: Setting Priorities in the Face of Decision Overload

1. Gail MacDonald, *Keep Climbing* (Wheaton: Tyndale, 1989), 29.
2. Karen Hutchcraft, "Love On the Front Lines," *Campus Life Leaders Guide* (February 1988): LG15.
3. Robert Crosby, "Balance, Bend, and Blend: Making Time For Family," *Campus Life Leaders Guide* (October 1988): LG15.

4. Ridge Burns, *Create in Me a Youth Ministry* (Wheaton: Victor, 1987), 117.
5. Quoted in MacDonald, *op.cit.*, 1.

Chapter Eleven Perseverance: Arming for the Sexual Battle

1. Anonymous, quoted in "Leadership at Its Best," *Leadership* (Winter Quarter 1990): 45.
2. Ibid.

Chapter Twelve Appraisal: A Sane View of Myself

1. Paul Tournier, *The Strong and the Weak* (Philadelphia: Westminster, 1964), 21.
2. Leroy Eims, *Be the Leader You Were Meant To Be* (Wheaton: Victor, 1975), 10-11.
3. Ibid., 24.

Chapter Thirteen Pacing: A Marathoner's Perspective

1. John Sanford, *Ministry Burnout* (New York: Paulist Press, 1982), 18.
2. Gail MacDonald, *Keep Climbing* (Wheaton: Tyndale, 1989), 33.
3. Robert J. Clinton, *The Making of a Leader* (Colorado Springs: NavPress, 1988), 218.

Chapter Fifteen Perspective: Time Alone With God

1. Dewey Bertolini, *Back to the Heart of Youth Work* (Wheaton: Victor Books, 1989), 23.
2. *Ibid.*, 23.
3. *Ibid.*, 29.
4. Concerts of prayer are two three-hour gatherings where people pray in a variety of contexts for the outpouring of God's Spirit. They are fashioned after ideas found in David

Bryant's *With Concerts of Prayer* (Glendale, California: Regal, 1984).

5. Bertolini, *op.cit.*, 19.

Chapter Seventeen Accountability: Who Is Keeping Me Honest?

1. Earl Palmer, "Who Needs a Mentor?" *Campus Life Leaders Guide* (April 1989): LG15.
2. *Ibid.*
3. J. David Stone, *Spiritual Growth in Youth Ministry* (Loveland, Colorado: GROUP, 1985), 45.

Conclusion Setting the Pace for Growth

1. J. David Stone, *Spiritual Growth in Youth Ministry* (Loveland, Colorado: GROUP, 1985), 24.